The Everyday Gourmet

The Joy
of Mediterranean Cooking

Bill Briwa, C.E.C., C.H.E.

PUBLISHED BY:

THE GREAT COURSES
Corporate Headquarters
4840 Westfields Boulevard, Suite 500
Chantilly, Virginia 20151-2299
Phone: 1-800-832-2412
Fax: 703-378-3819
www.thegreatcourses.com

Bill Briwa, C.E.C., C.H.E.
Chef-Instructor
The Culinary Institute of America
at Greystone

A 1980 graduate of The Culinary Institute of America (CIA), Chef Bill Briwa has worked in the hospitality industry for more than 30 years and is a Certified Executive Chef and Certified Hospitality Educator. In California's Napa Valley, he was the resident chef for The Hess Collection winery, owned and operated his own bistro, and worked at Thomas Keller's award-winning restaurant The French Laundry. He was also the executive chef for The Wine Spectator Restaurant at the CIA at Greystone and served as an officer on the board of the St. Helena Farmers' Market. As culinary chair of the 2004 Napa Valley Wine Auction, Chef Briwa helped raise more than five million dollars for local charities. In addition to his work as a chef, he has been both a baker and pastry chef. His writing on food and wine, olive oil, and cooking has been featured locally and in *Fine Cooking*, *Mise en Place*, and *Sunset*, as well as in the trade publications *Flavor & the Menu* and *Practical Winery & Vineyard Journal*.

As a Chef-Instructor at the CIA, Chef Briwa has developed curricula and has taught cooking, flavor dynamics, gastronomy, and food-and-wine pairing full time for the past 18 years. He has traveled to both teach and study cooking across the United States; in China, Mexico, South and Central America, and Europe; and around the Mediterranean. In addition, he is part of the Industry Services Group at the CIA and works closely with a broad range of corporate clients to help them identify and realize their culinary goals.

Chef Briwa has been a speaker at many professional conferences. He takes part in the Healthy Kitchens, Healthy Lives conference held each year at the CIA. The conference is copresented by the Harvard School of Public Health and the CIA. Chef Briwa has collaborated with Dr. Connie Guttersen, an instructor at the CIA and author of *The Sonoma*

Diet, on numerous presentations on nutrition and cooking, including a course on the science of healthy cooking produced by The Great Courses. In 2003, Chef Briwa was a judge for the American Cheese Society, and in 2005, he presented on gastronomy at the annual conference of the International Association of Culinary Professionals. In 2005, 2006, and 2007, he presented at the International Foodservice Manufacturers Association's Chain Operators Exchange conference, and in 2008 and 2009, he spoke at the National Restaurant Association Show in Chicago. Chef Briwa is an olive oil enthusiast; he presented at Beyond Extra Virgin IV, a conference on superpremium olive oil, in Verona, Italy.

Over the last 35 years of cooking and teaching, Chef Briwa has taken one short two-year break from the stove to become a puppeteer. He lives in Yountville, California, with his wife and a border collie—both of whom think highly of his cooking.

Chef Briwa is the instructor for four other offerings in The Great Courses' *Everyday Gourmet* series: *Rediscovering the Lost Art of Cooking, Making Healthy Food Taste Great, Making Great Meals in Less Time*, and *Essential Secrets of Spices in Cooking*. ■

Table of Contents

Table of Contents

Note to the Home Chef

The ingredient lists provided in this guidebook are for general reference only. Chef Briwa frequently substitutes or adds ingredients as he cooks and encourages you to do the same. The key to becoming a great chef is to learn about your ingredients and how they change in the process of cooking, to taste your food frequently as you develop a dish, and to be courageous enough to experiment in the kitchen.

Tastes of the Mediterranean

Lesson 1

The countries that rim the Mediterranean basin could not be more different from one another, but they do have common threads. Throughout this course, you will explore the countries that are the fabric of the Mediterranean, identifying the common threads woven into that fabric along the way. You will explore cooking traditions, techniques, and ingredients and tease apart the flavor profiles of Mediterranean food so that you can approach it with more understanding and confidence. In this lesson, you will learn how to cook some of the many small dishes that populate menus around the Mediterranean.

Pinchos Morunos (Grilled Pork with Sweet Spices and Flame Seedless Grapes)

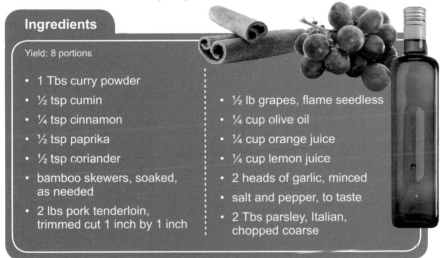

Ingredients

Yield: 8 portions

- 1 Tbs curry powder
- ½ tsp cumin
- ¼ tsp cinnamon
- ½ tsp paprika
- ½ tsp coriander
- bamboo skewers, soaked, as needed
- 2 lbs pork tenderloin, trimmed cut 1 inch by 1 inch

- ½ lb grapes, flame seedless
- ¼ cup olive oil
- ¼ cup orange juice
- ¼ cup lemon juice
- 2 heads of garlic, minced
- salt and pepper, to taste
- 2 Tbs parsley, Italian, chopped coarse

Pinchos morunos is a dish of skewered food—in this case, pork—in the style of the Moors. This is a tapa, which is a small dish from Spain, and it's probably one of the most popular.

A Grilling Tip

When you're grilling meat on skewers, often the meat will stick to the grill initially. Do not try to wrestle it free; instead, just let it sit and cook a little bit. As it cooks, some of the fat in the meat will rise to the surface of the meat, and the meat fibers will constrict, or pull back. As they do, they will pull themselves free of the grill, and then you should be able to turn the skewers pretty easily.

To make this dish, the first step is to make a marinade for the pork. This marinade is distinctive because it contains exotic spices, including curry powder, cumin, cinnamon, paprika, and coriander. Add garlic to the spice mixture, along with orange juice, lemon juice, and olive oil. Add salt and pepper to taste. Stir all of these ingredients together.

Then, put the marinade on the pork. Start by skewering a piece of pork tenderloin, which is a very tender cut of meat. Then, put a grape on the skewer, followed by another piece of meat, and continue alternating like this until all of your skewers are full.

Spoon the marinade on top of the skewers, and let them sit in the marinade for 20 to 30 minutes. Once the meat has marinated,

A History Lesson

In 1492, when Columbus was busy discovering America, the Spaniards won their independence from the North African Moors, who had ruled Spain for about 700 years. During that time, they brought agriculture, architecture, commerce, and astronomy to Spain. In terms of culinary influences, they brought exotic spices from the Middle and Far East.

Pinchos morunos probably would have been eaten originally by the Moors with lamb, because they have a religious prohibition against the consumption of pork. When the Moors were forced out of Spain and the Spaniards won their independence, the Spaniards made that same dish of skewered meat with exotic spices that the Moors had brought over, but the Spaniards instead used pork, a meat the Moors would never dream of eating, as a symbol of their independence.

you're going to cook it. Place the skewers on a hot grill. Once the skewers are cooked all the way through and have some nice browning on them, turn off the heat of the grill.

A rustic dish like this benefits from some coarsely chopped parsley. When you're ready to serve the skewers, put a little bit of chopped parsley on top of the skewers, along with a drizzle of fresh lemon juice.

Brandade of Salt Cod

Ingredients

Yield: 12 tapas

- ½ lb salt cod
- 1 cup milk
- ½ lb potatoes, Russet or Yukon Gold, pulp, cooked
- 2 oz cream, heavy
- 2 cloves garlic, peeled and minced
- 1 oz shallots, peeled and minced

- 1 lemon, juiced
- ½ tsp espelette pepper
- 1 ½ cups extra-virgin olive oil
- 1 cup bread crumbs, fresh
- 1 Tbs anchovies, rinsed and chopped into a paste
- 1 Tbs parsley, chopped

Brandade of salt cod is often eaten in the south of France, but you'll also find it eaten in Spain, Italy, and Greece. Salt cod is a very popular fish. The fish is

The Technique of Salting Fish

While salt cod is popular all around the Mediterranean, most of it comes from the Americas. Basque fishermen on the Atlantic coast of the Iberian Peninsula sailed across the Atlantic—possibly even before Columbus discovered the Americas—and fished off the maritime states of New England and Canada. Along the way, they learned the technique of salting fish from the Scandinavians. This technique is one of the reasons that open-sea exploration could take place, because now there was a dependable supply of protein that fishermen could take with them, even if the fishing wasn't good.

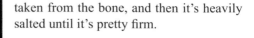

taken from the bone, and then it's heavily salted until it's pretty firm.

In Greece, this type of fish used to be known as "mountain fish," because it was really the only fish that you could eat if you were living away from the coast. As a way of preserving fish, the method of filleting it and salting it was tremendously practical.

To make this dish, the first thing you want to do is rinse the salt cod in the sink to get the loose salt off of the outside. Then, it needs to be soaked for about 24 hours. Cover it in water, and then put it into the refrigerator. Change the water three or four times within that 24 hours. After 24 hours, taste it, like you would taste a piece of cured meat. It shouldn't be overly salty; if it's overly salty, then it needs to be soaked for even longer.

Poach the soaked salt cod in milk. If there's any fishiness left, poaching it in milk will make it sweeter. Take the fish out of the milk when it flakes apart easily; that's how you'll know it's done. Put gloves on to flake the fish apart, keeping your eye open for anything objectionable, including bones and skin. Then, put the fish into a food processor.

In a pan on the stove, sauté some shallots and garlic in olive oil very gently until they are aromatic and translucent. Then, add this to the food processor as well.

Next, puree the cod in the food processor. This shouldn't take very long because the fish should be pretty tender already. But you might notice that it's a little bit fibrous now.

The next step is to add some cooked potatoes to the mixture in the food processor. Add the same amount of potatoes as there is salt cod in the processor and puree the mixture again. But once the potatoes go in, just pulse the processor, because too much activity can make potatoes turn gluey.

Then, introduce some cream. The goal is to make the mixture light, almost a mousse-like consistency. In some ways, it should feel like you're making mashed potatoes.

Taste the mixture. You should be able to taste the garlic and shallots. Add salt and pepper as needed. If you have it, espelette pepper is a great Spanish pepper that is often used in this dish. It's not too hot, but it lends a nice color and flavor. When you taste the mixture, if it's still a little bit rich because of all the cream, add a squeeze of lemon juice to it as well.

Put the mixture into a gratin dish. Toss fresh bread crumbs with a little bit of olive oil, allowing the oil to soak into the bread crumbs. Cover the mixture with the bread crumbs. Then, pop the dish into the oven at 375 degrees for about 10 minutes, until the crumbs brown and the brandade becomes hot and begins to soufflé. When you're ready to serve this dish, sprinkle some parsley on top, along with some anchovies, if desired. Bring it to your table with some olive oil toast and a glass of wine.

Dolmas

Ingredients

Yield: 32 dolmas

- 1 cup long-grain rice
- 5 oz ground lamb
- 2 Tbs olive oil
- 1 small onion, chopped fine
- 3 cloves of garlic, minced
- 1 tsp cinnamon
- 1 tsp allspice
- 3 oz tomatoes, diced
- 2 Tbs pine nuts, toasted
- 3 Tbs currants, plumped
- 1 ½ Tbs dill
- 1 ½ Tbs mint
- 1 ½ Tbs parsley, chopped
- 1 jar of grape leaves, drained and rinsed
- 1 qt vegetable or chicken stock
- salt and pepper, to taste
- 1 lemon, juiced
- 1 bay leaf
- 2 branches of thyme
- ⅓ cup extra-virgin olive oil

Dolmas are stuffed grape leaves. You'll find them in abundance in Greece, but also in Turkey in the eastern Mediterranean. If you were to draw a line from north to south in the Mediterranean, falling between Italy and Greece, rice is a pretty big deal to the east of that line. To the west of that line, you see a lot more wheat in the form of bread or pasta. In the eastern Mediterranean, you may find grape leaves that are stuffed with bulgur wheat, but rice is traditionally used in this recipe.

To make dolmas, the first step is to cook some diced onions and garlic in a pan with hot oil. Start by cooking just the onions in the oil until they are translucent, at which point all of the harsh, sulfurous compounds that some people find burning on their palate have been driven off. You don't want the onions to brown; turn the temperature down if you start to see some color. There's a sweetness that comes out of onions that have been cooked in this way. Once you begin to smell that sweetness, it's time to add the garlic. As soon as you can smell the garlic, that means it's done cooking.

Next, add some ground lamb to the pan, and cook it until it is browned. You could use a small amount of trim that is left over from a roast of lamb or maybe the shank meat that is a little bit too tough to roast.

In this dish, the lamb is like a condiment or flavoring agent. This dish is not grape leaves stuffed with lamb; it's grape leaves stuffed with rice. The lamb just lends a certain amount of flavor and depth. In the Mediterranean, a small amount of meat often is used to flavor nutrient-dense food.

Once the meat is browned, add allspice and cinnamon to the pan. Simmering these two spices in the hot fat will bring them to life. When you start to smell them, turn the burner off.

To make the filling for the grape leaves, start by soaking long-grain rice for about 30 to 60 minutes. It can be challenging to get the rice cooked once it's wrapped in the grape leaves, so this starts the process of softening the rice. Be careful: Once the rice is soaked, it's possible to break it, and you want the rice grains to be whole.

After soaking the rice, drain the water. Then, add the meat, onions, garlic, and spices to the rice. Next, add some chopped tomatoes. Brown some pine nuts either in the oven or on top of the stove in a small amount of oil. Add the browned pine nuts to the rice. Allow some currants to plump up in a little bit of hot water. Add the plumped currants to the rice. Also add a little bit of lemon juice.

Finally, add dill, parsley, and mint to this preparation. Stir everything together. Season the mixture with a little bit of salt and pepper. At this point, the rice is not cooked, but it is a good idea to taste it to make sure that it has the right amount of salt. The rice is going to be crunchy, but you can evaluate the salt content and correct it if necessary.

Now that the filling is done, it is time to stuff it into grape leaves. If you have a grapevine outside your house, you can strip some leaves from the vine; alternatively, you can buy jarred grape leaves. If the leaves come from a jar, they might have a little bit of the stem attached. Take a pair of scissors and snip those off, because they tend to be a little bit tough. If you're lucky enough to have fresh grape leaves, you'll have to blanch them in boiling, salted water until they become a little bit tender. Otherwise, they won't roll as easily as the jarred leaves.

If you have torn leaves or leaves that are very small, set them aside. Don't try to use them as a wrapper, because that will only lead to frustration. Instead, use large grape leaves for wrapping.

Lay out about 30 to 35 grape leaves on a table. Divide the filling among the leaves, using a little less than a tablespoon in each one. When the rice begins to cook, it will swell, so you don't want to overstuff the leaves. If you see any big chunks of meat, just break them up so that each leaf gets some bits of meat.

Then, line up all of the grape leaves and start rolling them up. Bring the bottom of the leaf up and over the filling, fold the edges in over the filling, and then roll it all up.

Once you have rolled all of your grape leaves, the next step is to cook them in a shallow dish. In fact, you are going to poach them in vegetable or chicken stock. Start by lining the shallow dish with some of the smaller or torn grape leaves, if you have them. If you only have whole grape leaves, then use those. This lining will protect the grape leaves by keeping them from moving around too much in the boiling liquid.

Lay the stuffed grape leaves all the way around the outside of the dish, with the overlapped seam down to keep the leaves from unfurling while they cook. If you find that you have almost enough but not enough stuffed leaves to fill the dish, meaning that you have a large empty area in the middle of the dish, then find a small plate that will fit in the middle empty area to keep the stuffed leaves from moving around. Finally, cover the stuffed grape leaves with more grape leaves, which will hold the stuffed leaves in place as they're cooking.

In a pot on the stove, heat vegetable or chicken stock. Add a few branches of thyme, a bay leaf, and some lemon juice. Season the broth almost like you would season a soup. Taste the broth, adding salt and pepper as needed. Once the liquid is hot, add it to the shallow dish containing the stuffed grape leaves. Add enough so that the grape leaves are completely covered with liquid. Then, bring the liquid to a simmer. Turn the heat down and maintain a low simmer with a lid on top.

Instead of cooking this on top of the stove, to free up some space you can put it into the oven at about 350 degrees for about an hour. You know the stuffed grape leaves are done when you cut one open and the rice on the inside is tender.

Once the stuffed grape leaves are done cooking, drain the braising liquid. If you save the braising liquid, you can add it to a soup later, or you can use it to make dolmas again at another point in the future. The liquid will only be tastier after having been used to cook this batch of grape leaves.

You can enjoy dolmas in a few different ways. You can serve them hot, in which case you can use the braising liquid as a sauce. You can also serve them cold, in which case having a yogurt sauce to go with them is a good idea. You can even just drizzle them with a little olive oil.

Dates with Pecorino, Arugula, and Cracked Pepper

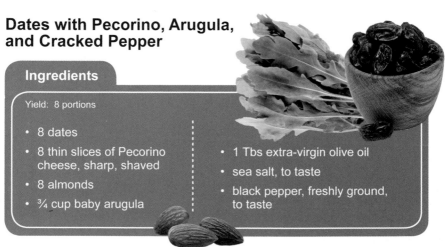

Ingredients

Yield: 8 portions

- 8 dates
- 8 thin slices of Pecorino cheese, sharp, shaved
- 8 almonds
- ¾ cup baby arugula

- 1 Tbs extra-virgin olive oil
- sea salt, to taste
- black pepper, freshly ground, to taste

You might find this appetizer—which features dates, Pecorino cheese, and almonds—in Sicily and southern Italy. To make this appetizer, start by cutting part of the way through the dates in order to open them up and pull out the pit. You don't want to be too aggressive, because you want the dates to hold their shape. Then, use a vegetable peeler to shave a few slices of the Pecorino cheese. Then, tuck a piece or two of the cheese into the date, and then tuck an almond in there as well. Set the stuffed date aside and repeat the process with another date.

Pecorino Cheese

The designation "Pecorino" refers to all sheep's milk cheeses. Sheep's milk cheeses and goat's milk cheeses have about seven to nine percent butterfat, so they are much richer than cow's milk cheeses, which have only about three-and-a-half percent butterfat. In addition, goat and sheep can eke out an existence on a scrubby hillside, whereas cattle really need pasture land or forage, so the cheeses that come from goat and sheep are more interesting, because you can taste the wild herbs and vegetation that the animals eat.

Present the stuffed dates on a bed of arugula, which has a pepperiness that tastes almost like you topped the dates with fresh ground pepper and a nuttiness that speaks to the almonds. Sprinkle the dish with a little bit of salt. Finally, drizzle some good extra-virgin olive oil on top. You could have this appetizer with a glass of wine before a meal—or with a glass of sherry if you're eating Spanish food.

Butter and Cheese—
Northern Italy

Lesson 2

Italy was once a series of small city-states, and there are pockets of regional cuisine that remain distinct from one another. In this lesson, you will learn about the cuisine of northern Italy. The long country of Italy spans many different climates, and northern Italy is so cold that the olive tree does not flourish. This is one of the reasons that northern Italian food bears more similarities to northern European food than to typical Mediterranean food. In addition, the Mediterranean is rocky, dry, and arid and without much pastureland, but northern Italy has pastureland. This is why meat, veal, dairy, butter, and cream are staples in northern Italian cuisine.

Ricotta Gnocchi

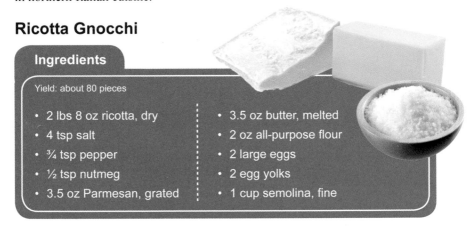

Ingredients

Yield: about 80 pieces

* 2 lbs 8 oz ricotta, dry
* 4 tsp salt
* ¾ tsp pepper
* ½ tsp nutmeg
* 3.5 oz Parmesan, grated

* 3.5 oz butter, melted
* 2 oz all-purpose flour
* 2 large eggs
* 2 egg yolks
* 1 cup semolina, fine

This dish starts with ricotta cheese, which is a by-product of cheese making. The whey that's left over is recooked, and at a higher temperature, more curd comes out. You can drain ricotta overnight in cheesecloth to make it a little drier.

To make this dish, start by flavoring the ricotta with a little bit of Parmesan cheese and some fresh nutmeg (if you have ground nutmeg in a container, that's fine). Then, season it with salt and pepper. You are going to use egg and flour to bind everything together. Add one whole egg and one egg yolk, which lends some richness to the gnocchi. Start the process of mixing everything up. Then, add a small amount of flour.

As you're mixing, try to make the dough smooth and homogeneous, making sure that the seasonings get transferred to all parts of the dough. You shouldn't see any streaks of egg or flour that have not been moistened. When everything

seems to be mixed well, taste the dough to determine if it has enough nutmeg, Parmesan, salt, and pepper, and adjust the flavors as necessary. Finally, to enrich the dough, add some melted butter, and mix it in as well.

The next step involves shaping the gnocchi. Take a little knob of the dough onto a cutting board and shape it into a log. Roll the dough and coat the outside of it with semolina flour (or regular flour), which not only keeps the dough from sticking to the board but also absorbs excess moisture that forms on the outside of the dough. If your log gets too long, just break it in half. Roll the log down to about three-quarters of an inch thick, and then cut it into small pieces.

Semolina Flour

Semolina, which means "semi-milled," is a flour that is yellow in color. The yellow color of semolina comes from the fact that durum wheat, which is the wheat that is ground into semolina, has a creamy yellow color that makes pastas look like they have a lot more egg in them than they actually do.

Move the cut pieces of gnocchi onto a plate or pan to store them until you're ready to cook them. While transferring the gnocchi, give them a little squeeze in the middle to form a small indented waist. This not only makes them look more interesting but also helps them cook a little more evenly.

Before you shape all of your gnocchi, test a few in a pot of boiling, salted water. When you drop them in, they will drop to the bottom of the pot, which tells you that they're relatively dense, but as they cook, they will rise up to the surface. Let the gnocchi gently simmer; you don't want them to boil really hard.

Then, your test pieces of gnocchi should be taken out of the water, and you can evaluate their texture. If they are too loose and tend to fall apart, add a little more flour or some extra egg white to your unshaped dough to help bind the gnocchi together. If the test pieces are too tight and tough, add a little more melted butter or a little milk to the dough to help loosen them up.

Once the gnocchi are shaped, they can sit in the refrigerator for an hour or two, or you can even freeze them for later. It's a benefit if you can let them sit for a an hour or two, because any excess moisture will be absorbed by the semolina on the outside, and it will create a little bit of a shell that will help hold the gnocchi together.

While the gnocchi sits in the refrigerator, prepare your sauce. You can serve gnocchi in many different ways. Maybe the simplest way to serve them is topped with tomato sauce, but they are also great with vegetables. Different times of the year offer different vegetables; use what's in season.

As an example, you can use zucchini and cherry tomatoes. Cut the zucchini into thin ribbons, which allows them to cook very quickly. Cut the cherry tomatoes in half so that they're not quite so large and also so that some of the liquid can begin the process of turning itself into a fresh tomato sauce.

Next, add some butter to a hot pan. Then, add a little bit of the salted pasta water you used to test your gnocchi. This will make a very simple sauce, in which you can cook the zucchini and tomatoes. In the bottom of the pan, you should see a sauce start to form, composed of the butter and the juices from the tomatoes. Season it with salt and pepper.

Basil

Basil turns black if you chop it, so the best way of handling it is to roll it up into a little cigar and cut it into ribbons.

Finally, add a portion or two of the gnocchi to the boiling, salted water. Pasta likes a lot of water, so use a big pot and a good amount of salt. Once the gnocchi are done cooking, remove them from the pot and ease them, piece by piece, into the pan with the sauce, just to warm them up slightly. Sauce can be basted on top of them. Taste the gnocchi for salt, and add some basil to the pan. Sprinkle with Parmesan cheese before serving.

Vitello Tonnato
(Cold Veal with Tuna Sauce)

Ingredients

Yield: 10 portions

Veal

- 1 ½ lbs veal loin, tied, seasoned

Tonnato sauce

- 2 oz onion, diced
- 1 oz carrot, diced
- 1 oz celeriac, diced
- 2 Tbs olive oil
- 1 Tbs tomato paste
- ½ tsp garlic, minced
- 3 tsp capers, drained
- 4 anchovy fillets
- ¼ cup lemon juice

- ½ cup white wine
- 1 cup brown beef or veal stock
- 1 sachet d'épices (bay leaf, cracked pepper, thyme sprig, and rosemary sprig)
- 2 oz canned imported tuna, or tuna confit

Garnish

- 1 red onion, sliced paper thin
- 10 capers, drained and rinsed
- 10 anchovy fillets

13

Vitello tonnato, or veal with tuna sauce, is a great summer dish. To make this dish, start by cleaning a piece of veal loin completely. Veal loin has some connective tissue that you want to get underneath with your knife and remove. Because you're going to roast the meat, you should truss it, or tie it up, so that it holds a uniform shape and roasts as a solid piece of meat. Once the meat is trussed, it's ready to be roasted.

First, season the meat with salt and pepper. Put it into a pan with a little bit of olive oil, and brown it first on top of the stove before you put in the oven at 350 degrees. A piece of meat that is about two inches thick will probably roast for about 15 to 18 minutes. After this time, if you squeeze the meat, it should still be a little soft on the inside. A meat thermometer inserted into it should read about 140 to 145 degrees. The veal should be allowed to cool, because this dish is served cold.

The next step is to make a sauce for the veal. In a hot pan, sauté celery, carrots, and onions—the foundational vegetables used in most of northern European cooking. This recipe calls for celery root (celeriac), which is a little starchy, so it'll help thicken the sauce slightly. If you don't have celery root, you can use green celery. Also add a few cloves of garlic to the pan. Because all of the vegetables will be strained out, you can just flatten the garlic cloves and add them whole. Brown the vegetables for about three or four minutes.

Once you see the onions start to brown, add some capers and a few anchovy fillets to the pan. Mash the fillets against the hot pan so that they begin to

break down. Then, add a little tomato paste; take the time to brown it just a little bit. Once the tomato paste turns to kind of a brick red color (versus its original bright red color), deglaze the pan with a little bit of white wine by turning up the heat so that the liquid reduces down almost dry.

Once the white wine has reduced, add some beef stock. Alternatively, you could add veal stock. The pan that you cooked the veal in should have a glaze on the bottom. In French tradition, this is called the fond, or foundation; it's basically meat essence that has collected on the bottom of the pan. If you heat the pan and then introduce a little bit of water, you should be able to scrape all of that goodness out of the bottom of the pan. (Do not do this if the fond in the pan was burned.) Then, add this to the sauce instead of beef stock. Simmer for about 15 to 20 minutes.

While the sauce is reducing, add a bay leaf, cracked pepper, thyme, and rosemary. The herbs will flavor the sauce as it cooks down. There's no need to chop the herbs; they're going to be strained out later.

Once the liquid is reduced to about three-quarters of a cup, or six ounces, strain out the solids. Press all the flavor out of the vegetables. Once the solids have been removed, add about a quarter of a cup of mayonnaise to the liquid.

Finally, it's time to add the tuna element, which comes from canned tuna packed in olive oil. Puree a few ounces of tuna in a food processor, or, for more texture, break down the tuna with the back of a spoon. Add it to the sauce.

Brighten the sauce with a little bit of lemon juice, and perhaps a drop or two of water if you want the sauce to be slightly thinner.

The last step is to cut the piece of veal you roasted earlier. Make sure that you cut all of the strings that had been tied on the meat. The veal should be cold now, so it should slice very easily with a sharp knife. Slice it fairly thin; this is a tender piece of meat and a delicate preparation. Spoon the sauce over the entire surface of the meat before serving.

As a garnish, slice up a lemon, which can be squeezed on this dish according to taste. Also garnish with capers, or even some caper berries if you have them. Shaved red onion is another garnish that goes well with this dish, along with some anchovy fillets.

Tiramisu

Ingredients

Yield: 1 dessert

- 4 Tbs espresso coffee
- 1 Tbs rum
- 1 Tbs brandy
- 1 Tbs Kahlúa
- 3 eggs, separated

- ½ cup sugar
- 8 oz marscapone cheese
- 24 ladyfinger sponge cookies
- 1 oz sweet chocolate, grated

Tiramisu is a simple Italian dessert of ladyfingers that are moistened with espresso coffee. Spirits are added to the coffee to give it a little kick.

Start with the espresso. To it, add some brandy, dark rum, and Kahlúa. You can add a different combination of spirits, if you'd like; the only real requirement is that you like the taste of the mixture of coffee and spirits.

The next step is to separate the whites and the yolks of three eggs. Using a whisk, whip the yokes with some sugar for about a minute or a minute and a half. Adding the sugar will lighten the yolks both in color and in texture. You want the mixture to become homogenous; you want the sugar to dissolve.

Once the yolks are lighter and begin to hold some air, fold them into some mascarpone cheese, which is basically an Italian cream cheese. But while most cream cheeses in America tend to be firm, mascarpone is very delicate and very rich. Add the yolk mixture in two parts: The first addition will begin the

process of lightening the mascarpone; when it's almost uniform, with very few streaks in it, then fold in the rest of the yolk mixture.

With a clean whisk, whip up the egg whites. You want them to be shiny and moist but starting to firm up just a little bit. If they get too dry and stiff, then when you try to fold them in, they won't fold smoothly. Fold the egg whites into the mascarpone mixture slowly, in three parts. The first will lighten the mixture considerably, but a lot of the air will be knocked out. When it is almost all incorporated, add the second third, which will hold slightly more air. Finally, add the last third. Fold the egg whites in just until you see no more streaks of egg white.

Use a glass bowl to build the tiramisu. Start with a layer of ladyfingers in the bottom of the dish. Before you add another layer of cookies, moisten them with some of the coffee mixture. Make sure the cookies absorb a good amount of the coffee and spirits. Then, add some of the mascarpone mixture. Add a second layer of ladyfingers, coffee, and mascarpone. The topping is the second layer of mascarpone.

Put the tiramisu into the refrigerator for about five to six hours, or even overnight. Before serving, grate some chocolate over the top of the tiramisu.

Classical Italian Cuisine— Central Italy

Lesson 3

C entral Italy is where classical cooking in Italy got its start. The weather in central Italy is mild enough that the olive tree can flourish, but it's not so mild that you don't have to pay attention. In Tuscany, for example, olives have to be harvested before the first hard frost, or even snow, because the olives will be lost if they are frozen. The early harvest results in a greener oil, and the cuisine lines up behind that oil, using bitter greens and big flavors. In this lesson, you will learn how to make handmade pappardelle, ragù Bolognese, a three-colored salad, and a simple soup called *stracciatelle*.

Handmade Pappardelle

Ingredients

Yield: 15 portions

All-purpose pasta dough

- 1 lb pasta flour
  (¾ lb all-purpose flour and
  ¼ lb semolina or durum flour)

- 4 eggs, beaten
- water (enough to make 8 oz of liquid when combined with eggs)

Pappardelle is pasta that looks like wide ribbons. To make handmade pappardelle, first set up a food processor. Add about a pound of a blend of all-purpose flour and durum flour, which is a hard wheat flour. Wheat flour contains a lot of gluten, a mixture of proteins that becomes very elastic and strong when mixed with water. That strength is what allows the pasta to withstand the rigors of being rolled, cut, and ultimately cooked.

Turn on the food processor, and begin to add about four eggs to the flour blend. The goal is to form dough that resembles moist sand that begins to cascade on itself. You don't want it to form a ball of dough the way you might if you were making bread in a food processor. Once the dough looks like wet sand, take it out and give it a squeeze. It should be moist enough to bind together.

Gather the mixture into a single piece of dough, and knead the dough by sending it through the rollers of a pasta machine and then folding it on itself and putting it back through the rollers. This, in effect, will mimic kneading, a

process that makes the dough stronger. Continue putting the dough through the machine until it becomes very smooth and cohesive.

As the dough begins to develop and becomes more elastic, it may be more difficult to roll it through the rollers. When you get to that point, roll it through once at the widest setting, and then roll it through again at a narrower setting so that it becomes longer and thinner, and then open it back up and fold it onto itself.

Once the dough is firm and smooth, let it relax for a little while. Allowing the gluten to relax means that you can roll the dough through the machine without it tearing. Once the pasta is all rolled out, cut it into pieces that are about 10 to 12 inches long. Before you begin to stack up pieces of pasta, put a little flour on the dough because you don't want it to stick together. Then, cut it into ribbons that are about half an inch thick.

For the first 30 minutes after you've cut your pasta, periodically give it a little stir, making sure that it's loose and hasn't stuck to itself. After 30 minutes have passed, it will have dried out to the point where you don't have to worry about it anymore. The pasta will sit very happily from the day you make it until the following day, but if you want to keep it without cooking it for longer than that, you should probably freeze it because it has eggs in it.

Ragù Bolognese

Ingredients

Yield: 6–8 portions

- ½ cup heavy cream
- 10 oz pancetta, diced small
- 1 qt water
- 1 cup carrot, diced
- ⅔ cup celery, diced
- ½ cup onion, diced
- 1 ¼ lbs beef skirt steak (or boneless chuck blade roast)

- ½ cup Italian white wine, preferably Trebbiano or Albana
- 2 Tbs Italian tomato paste (double or triple concentrated), diluted in 10 Tbs veal or beef stock
- 1 cup whole milk
- 1 tsp salt
- ¼ tsp ground black pepper

A sauce from central Italy called ragù Bolognese, or meat sauce, is a great sauce to make with pappardelle. The sauce starts with some pancetta in a hot pan. Cook the pancetta and render all of the fat. Once the fat has come out of it, brown some onions, carrots, and celery in the fat. The pancetta left behind a little film of goodness on the bottom of the pan, called the fond. The juices that came from the pork evaporated their liquid and ended up clinging to the pan. As you introduce this bunch of vegetables, they bring a certain amount of moisture with them that, in effect, frees that film on the pan. You're deglazing with vegetables.

Once you notice the onions turning translucent and starting to take on just a little bit of color, you're going to add beef to the pan. Dice up the beef about a quarter of an inch on a side. You can use skirt steak, but any rich cut would be appropriate, including shank meat, shoulder meat, and chuck.

By adding the meat to the pan, you're introducing moisture again. The water in the meat comes out and deglazes the pan. The water reduces, and when it's all gone, then the temperature can rise, and the food begins to brown. Cook the meat for about 10 minutes, or until it begins to brown. Don't cook it so long that it becomes dry, crusty, and overly brown.

Once the meat begins to brown, you'll notice that meat juices have clung to the bottom of the pan. Before they burn, it's important to free them by deglazing with some white wine. The liquid in the pan cleans up all of the meat juices that have clung to the bottom. As the liquid disappears, the sound of the sizzling changes.

Once the liquid is gone, the next ingredient you're going to add is tomato paste. Briefly sauté the tomato paste in the pan and then thin it out with some veal or beef stock. From this point forward, it's important that this cooks very slowly.

You want the meat to get tender, but you don't want to add a lot of liquid, which will water down the flavor of the meat. So, the meat should be barely covered with stock.

To slow down how quickly the moisture can evaporate, make a cartouche, which is a little paper lid that is made by folding a piece of paper in half, and then in half again, and then in half again. Then, you measure how big the lid needs to be to fit your pan, and you tear off the part that you need. Put this little paper lid right on top of the meat.

Turn the heat down to a very low simmer. You should also put the lid that fits the pan on top so that the meat can cook gently. The stock will continue to reduce, little by little, over a period of about 45 minutes, and then the stock will be almost gone. From that point forward, you gently add small amounts of milk, keeping the meat moist but not soupy. You can also season it with salt and pepper.

After about two hours, the meat should be tender. Check the meat to make sure it is cooked. With each addition of milk along the way, the meat sauce becomes a little bit creamier. It should not be soupy. It should be relatively firm, so turn up the heat if you need to thicken it.

You want to finish the meat sauce with some heavy cream. Before adding the cream, reduce it in a separate pan by about one-half to two-thirds. You want the cream to become much thicker before you add it.

Now is the time to put some pappardelle in a pot

with salted, boiling water. Fresh pasta takes only about four minutes to cook, about half the time it takes to cook pasta from a box.

From this point on, you should pay attention to the consistency of the ragù. Once it's fairly thick and almost holds its shape on a spoon, add the reduced cream to it, which will smooth it out.

Sometimes traditional recipes for ragù Bolognese include mushrooms, wild or cultivated, that are browned along with the meat. If you like mushrooms, this is one way of adding more complexity to this dish.

After draining the pasta, pile it on a plate and ladle the sauce on top of the pasta. Sprinkle some Parmesan cheese on the top to lend a savory element to this dish.

Bitter Greens Salad

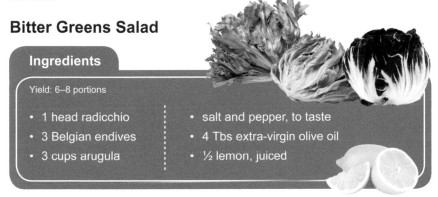

Ingredients

Yield: 6–8 portions

- 1 head radicchio
- 3 Belgian endives
- 3 cups arugula

- salt and pepper, to taste
- 4 Tbs extra-virgin olive oil
- ½ lemon, juiced

A great accompaniment to ragù Bolognese over handmade pappardale is a salad of bitter greens. The main dish is a fairly rich dish, and bitter greens act as a digestive. Americans tend to like sweet, tender baby lettuces, but Italians have a fondness for bitter greens.

Lettuces tend to wilt. They're mostly moisture, and as soon as they begin to lose water, they become tired and lackluster. But if you put them into cold water, they will become lively again. They will absorb water and become crisp. If you're serving a salad, you need to wash lettuces in cold water well in advance of your meal, then spin them dry or blot them dry with a towel, and finally put them in the refrigerator. The great thing about storing your greens for an hour or two in the refrigerator before your meal is that you can wrap them in a towel, and the towel will absorb all that excess moisture.

Start with radicchio, which is a bitter green that has reddish leaves. Cut a head of radicchio in half. Now that you can see the core, cut it out. Add the leaves to a salad bowl. Then, add a flavorful, nutty green: arugula. The final lettuce is Belgian endive, whose leaves are white instead of green.

Season the salad with salt and pepper. Then, dress it with a really punchy extra-virgin olive oil. The olive oils from Tuscany have a lot of complexity, pepperiness, bitterness, and pungency to them. You want to be generous with the olive oil, and then a little stingy with the lemon juice (or vinegar). Toss the salad in the bowl, and it's ready to be served.

Stracciatelle in Broth with Sorrel

Ingredients

Yield: 4 ½ cups

- 4 cups chicken broth
- Salt and pepper, to taste
- 1 large egg, cold
- 1 Tbs semolina flour

- 4 tsp Parmesan or Pecorino Romano
- 2 oz sorrel leaves, stems trimmed

With a complicated entree like ragù Bolognese over handmade pappardelle, you don't want to spend a lot of time preparing a first course. *Stracciatelle* is a simple soup that would be a great addition to this meal. It's a chicken broth that has little rags that are made up of egg. *Stracciatelle* is the same as egg drop soup that is served in an Asian restaurant.

To make this soup, add chicken broth to a pot on the stove, season it, and let it simmer. Then, in a separate bowl, whip an egg. You want to break up the structure of the egg so that it's homogeneous. Add some semolina flour to the egg, and whip it so that there are no lumps. Add some Parmesan cheese as well. Add the whipped egg to the soup, stirring it in.

Then, add some herbs, such as parsley or sorrel. If you use sorrel, cut it into ribbons. It has a wonderful lemony flavor, so the soup becomes very bright with the addition of sorrel. There's so much acid in sorrel that it almost purees itself when you put it into the soup. When the heat gets to it, it falls apart pretty quickly.

Taste the soup to make sure you're happy with the flavor before serving. Add salt and pepper as needed.

Bounty from the Sea— Southern Italy

Lesson 4

The end of the Italian peninsula is surrounded by water on three sides. Southern Italy, in particular, sticks out into the Mediterranean Sea. The climate is so hot in southern Italy that agriculture is incredibly abundant, and many varieties of produce are available. Similarly, the fishing is rich. In this lesson, you will learn about the cuisine of southern Italy by learning how to make caponata with seared tuna, margherita pizza, and coffee granita for dessert.

Caponata with Fennel-Crusted Tuna

Ingredients

Yield: 8 portions

Tuna
- 2 lbs tuna fillet
- ⅛ cup extra-virgin olive oil
- 2 Tbs fennel seed, ground
- salt and pepper, to taste

Caponata
- 2 eggplants, medium
- 1 cup olive oil
- 1 cup celery, diced
- 3 onions, chopped or sliced ¼-inch thick

- 1 cup tomato puree
- 3 Tbs capers, rinsed
- 12 black and green olives, pitted and chopped
- 4 Tbs pine nuts, toasted (or slivered almonds)
- ⅓ cup golden raisins
- ⅓ cup red wine vinegar
- 2 Tbs sugar

Caponata is an eggplant relish that comes from Sicily. To make it, start by adding olive oil and some onions to a hot pan on the stove. Once the onions are just about translucent, add some celery. In this dish, the celery should remain a little bit crisp, so don't put it in the pan at the same time as the onions.

Caponata features eggplant. Often, the eggplant is sautéed in oil and then taken out before the rest of the relish is made. But you can also dress the eggplant with a little bit of oil and then roast it in a hot oven. Eggplant loves to absorb

oil, and when you sauté it, sometimes this dish can become heavy. So, baking it in the oven is a good alternative.

Dice up the sautéed or roasted eggplant, with the skin on. The pieces of eggplant seem to hold together better if you leave the skin in place. To the hot pan, add capers, golden raisins, a blend of green and black olives, and toasted pine nuts. Stew all of this in some pureed tomato. Turn the heat down and let it simmer. At this point, you can add the cooked eggplant, which will absorb all of the flavors that are already in the pan.

Season the mixture in the pan with salt. Add some red wine vinegar to cut through the richness of the sautéed vegetables. Then, add some sugar. You want to find a balance between the acid of the red wine vinegar, the sweetness of the sugar, and the saltiness of the capers. Once you find that balance, pull the pan off the heat and let it cool.

Next, you're going to make some seared tuna to go with the caponata. Using a hot pan, you want to sear the tuna so that it gets some color on the outside without overcooking the inside. When you put tuna with spices on the outside into a hot pan, the spices will burn before you take the tuna out of the pan. So, don't add spices until later. But you can sprinkle salt on all four sides.

Turn the heat of your pan all the way up and introduce some oil. Then, the fish can be added to the pan. Be careful not to splash hot oil on yourself. The pan should be hot enough that the oil will begin to smoke almost immediately.

While the tuna is cooking on the first side, lay a piece of plastic wrap on your cutting board. Sprinkle the spices that you want on your piece of tuna on the plastic wrap. Use black pepper and some crushed fennel seed.

After about 20 to 30 seconds on the first side, turn the tuna to a new side, and cook it for another 20 to 30 seconds. Cook it for the same amount of time on each of the four sides. You want to keep it pretty rare inside, but the outsides should brown.

Once you have four nicely browned sides, take the tuna out of the pan and put it right onto the plastic wrap, rolling it back and forth a few times to make sure the spices are on the meat. To help the spices stick in place, wrap the tuna very briefly in the plastic wrap and let it sit and cool.

Unwrap the tuna from the plastic wrap, and with a very sharp knife, cut the tuna into slices. The interior of the tuna hasn't been salted yet, so sprinkle some salt on top of the slices of tuna. Lay the slices of tuna on a plate. The caponata, which should be cool by now, can be spooned onto the plate, along with some chopped parsley.

Pizza Dough

Ingredients

Yield: 4 individual pizzas

- 4 cups all-purpose flour
- 1 ½ cup water, warm
- 1 tsp salt

- 1 pkt yeast
- 3 Tbs extra-virgin olive oil

Southern Italy, especially Naples, is known for its pizza. Before you start the process of making a pizza, the first thing you should do is turn your oven up as high as it will go—probably around 500 degrees—and place a pizza stone in the oven. Allow the pizza stone to heat up for about an hour while you create your pizza.

The heart and soul of a good pizza is the dough. The ingredients are fairly simple: flour, yeast, salt, water, and olive oil. Start with the yeast. You'll need about a packet of yeast, or about two teaspoons. Add some warm water, about 100 to 110 degrees, to the yeast in a bowl. Set it aside and let it rise for about 10 minutes. It'll become kind of foamy. This process is called proofing. Much of the yeast that is sold in packages at the supermarket is called instant yeast, and it doesn't need to be proofed. You can just add it to your dough without going through this added step.

Add the yeast to some all-purpose flour. Never put salt in the water with the yeast. Salt and yeast don't like one another. Instead, wait until the yeast is already mixed into the dough before you add the salt. Don't add the oil yet, either, because the oil will encapsulate the yeast, and it won't be able to turn the flour into simpler starches that it digests and turns into carbon dioxide, which will then make the dough rise.

Flour and Gluten

Every flour has a certain amount of protein in it, what's known as gluten. When you add liquid to gluten and you manipulate it, it becomes elastic. That's what makes baked goods, including cakes and cookies, possible. A flour that has a lot of gluten is called a strong flour, and it can hold its shape in a large loaf. However, for something that you want to be very shallow, like pizza, use a flour like all-purpose flour, which only has about seven to nine percent protein.

Using a hand or stand mixer, start to mix the dough. Now you can add the salt, about a teaspoon. About halfway through the mixing, check on the dough. It should be a little sticky and moist. At this point, you might add a little bit of moisture or a little more flour if it needs it. Once the dough is almost fully mixed, add two tablespoons of oil to it.

After about eight minutes, take it out of the bowl and put it on the counter. Knead the dough, on a surface sprinkled with flour, until it becomes resilient, or elastic, and smooth. The mixer does the hard work for you, but you also want to knead the dough by hand by folding the dough over on itself and then rolling it forward. Add a little flour as needed, but be careful not to use too much.

One way of telling that the dough is fully kneaded is to take a little bit of it and begin to stretch it. Stretch it thinner and thinner, and it should become thin enough to be translucent before it tears. Once the dough is fully developed, put it in a bowl with a tablespoon of oil, coating the dough with the oil. Cover the dough with plastic wrap, and keep the bowl a warm spot to rise. In about an hour and a half, it will double in size. That's because the yeast is giving off carbon dioxide, and it's being trapped in the elastic matrix (the gluten) of the dough.

Once the dough has risen, you need to redistribute the yeast so that it can have more flour to digest. To do this, punch down through the middle of the dough, and then fold the edges over on top of the dough. After redistributing the yeast, you can divide the dough into four portions, which would be appropriate for about four individual pizzas.

Round the pieces of dough and set them aside to let them rise again. They need to sit for 20 to 30 minutes after you shape them so that they can relax and rise. The dough is ready to be used for pizza when it holds an indentation when you poke it.

Margherita Pizza

Ingredients

Yield: Two 9-inch pizzas

- pizza dough, two 6-oz balls
- unbleached all-purpose flour, cornmeal, or semolina for dusting pan
- ½ cup tomato sauce

- 16 basil leaves, fresh
- ¼ lb fresh mozzarella cheese
- 2 Tbs Parmesan or Pecorino Romano (or other dry, aged cheese), freshly grated, optional

Grab a piece of dough, being careful not to knock too much air out of it, and start the process of shaping a pizza. The first thing you want to do is press your fingers around the edge of the dough and create what will become the crust, a sort of crown. Then, press the insides a little, and pick the dough up and begin to stretch it. Feel for the spots where the dough is thick, and give some extra attention to those areas. Turn the dough over and stretch it over the back of your hands.

Little by little, your pizza shell will become rounder and bigger. An individual pizza size is around 9 or 10 inches. Once your dough is about that size, transfer it to a pan that is sprinkled with flour so that the dough slides off easily when you're ready to put it on a pizza stone.

To make the simplest pizza, margherita, start by spreading tomato sauce up to the edge of the dough without covering the crust. Tear a few basil leaves into pieces and sprinkle them over the crust. Then, cut some fresh mozzarella into slices and top the dough with them. Sprinkle some grated Parmesan or Pecorino cheese and some pepper on top. Exercise restraint. The pizza shouldn't be so loaded with ingredients that the dough can't bake.

Make sure that your oven is as hot as possible. The pizza stone you placed in the oven when you started making your pizza should be very hot—it holds a tremendous amount of heat. Move the pizza stone up toward the top of the oven. Because you also want a lot of heat on top of the pizza, you are going to switch the oven from the "bake" to the "broil" setting once the pizza is in the oven.

In one quick motion, carefully slide the pizza from the pan onto the hot pizza stone. Keep your eyes on the pizza; you don't want it to burn. You will start to see some signs that the pizza is cooking: The crown around the edge will begin to puff up, and the cheese will begin to soften. The crust will start to brown. Many people believe that a pizza crust should not just be golden brown but actually charred in spots.

After about six minutes, pull the pizza out to check it. You want to see a little bit of charring on the dough. The cheese should be browned in some spots. The bottom of the crust should be firm, and maybe a little brown. You can cook the pizza to your liking; these are just general guidelines.

Coffee Granita with Whipped Cream

Ingredients

Yield: 6 portions

- 4 cups espresso coffee
- 6 Tbs sugar

- ¾ cup whipped cream, sweetened

In the Mediterranean when the weather is hot, a dessert is not only a delicious sweet at the end of a meal, but it also cools you off. Granita is a frozen dessert that doesn't require an ice cream freezer to make it.

To make coffee granita, start by making some really strong coffee. You can also use espresso. Pour the coffee into a shallow pan. Then, add some sugar. The sugar plays two important roles: It tempers the bitterness of the coffee and keeps the liquid coffee from freezing solid. Instead, the sugar makes it freeze a little bit softer.

Once the sugar is dissolved, put the coffee mixture into the freezer for two or three hours. Once the granita is frozen, draw a fork over the top of it to shave it into a soft, crumbly, flaky, frozen convection, almost like a slush. You could use a food processor instead if you'd like.

Spoon some granita into a bowl. Drop a dollop of sweetened cream on the top, perhaps along with a few mint leaves, and serve.

The Everyday Joys of Olive Oil

Lesson 5

Olive oil is one of the most important ingredients in defining Mediterranean food. As you move away from the Mediterranean and the climate changes, the olive tree falters, and the cooking is no longer defined as Mediterranean. It's worthwhile to understand olive oil in the context of food, because it is central to Mediterranean cooking. As you will learn in this lesson, olive oil can make a variety of nutrient-dense food taste delicious—and it's delicious in its own right.

How Olive Oil Is Made

Olive oil begins with olives. Olives ripen in the fall. If the fruit is harvested when it's fully formed and green, when it is crushed, the oil is very green, peppery, and even a little bitter. But if the olive is allowed to stay on the tree after it's fully formed, the oil is soft, buttery, and maybe a little greasy.

Along the ripeness continuum, the yield increases. Of course, olive oil producers want to maximize yield, but they also want to maximize flavor—which is found earlier in the season. The challenge is to balance flavor and yield.

Once the olives are harvested, first they are washed, and then they are separated from sticks, twigs, seeds, and leaves. Next, they are crushed. This was traditionally done in a stone mill, but today it's done with a hammer mill, which is like a giant garbage disposal that creates a paste. That paste is then mixed for a short amount of time. The mixing allows the emulsion that may have formed in the crushing to break, and the oil begins to separate from the solids.

Ultimately, the goal is to separate the oil from everything else. Traditionally, this was done by spreading the paste onto hemp mats, stacking the mats up, and pressing them. The mat would capture the solids while the oil and water flowed out. The oil and water separated naturally, and the olive oil could be decanted off the top. Today, something similar to a cream separator, a centrifuge, spins the mixture. Because the oil is less dense than water, it will spin off at a different time, and the oil can be separated from water and from solids.

Tasting Olive Oil

While you can learn about olive oil from tasting it just as it is, understanding the flavor of olive oil in the context of food—which can be as simple as tasting it on a piece of bread—makes more sense. One way of doing this is to organize a tasting of three different extra-virgin olive oils by using them as dressings on salad. For example, you might try one from France, one from Spain, and one from Italy.

To do an olive oil tasting exercise, put together three small salads of shaved fennel, shaved endive, shaved mushrooms, and shaved Parmesan cheese. Dress each of the salads with a different olive oil. Season all three with salt and a few drops of lemon juice. Then, taste each salad, noting the differences in the flavors of the olive oils.

Another way of understanding olive oil in the context of food is to dip a piece of bread into the first olive oil you want to taste and then into a particular Mediterranean spice. This can be repeated with other olive oils and different spices. In the eastern Mediterranean, a number of different spice preparations are used as seasoning agents, two of which are *dukkah* and *za'atar*. *Dukkah* is made from cumin, coriander, nuts (almonds or hazelnuts), and sesame. *Za'atar* is made from wild thyme, sesame, and sumac (a souring agent used in that part of the world). If you were having an olive oil tasting party, or if you were inviting people to your home to enjoy Mediterranean food, these spices would be a great addition.

Whole Fish in an Aromatic Salt Crust

Ingredients

Yield: 6 portions

Salt mixture

- 2 lbs rock salt
- 1 lb kosher salt
- ¼ cup fennel seed, coarsely ground (may substitute aniseed)
- ¼ cup star anise, crushed
- 1 lemon, zested
- 1 orange, zested
- 2 oz egg whites

Fish

- 3 lbs fish, whole and dressed
- 3–4 thyme branches/parsley
- orange/lemon slices from above citrus

To make this dish, start with branzino, which you can buy from the fishmonger "pan dressed," which means that it's already gutted. All the fins have been trimmed, and it's been scaled.

First, stuff the fish's cavity with some herbs, including thyme and parsley. Then, add a few slices of lemon and a few slices of orange.

For this dish, you want to bake the fish inside of a crust of salt, which will keep the moisture in the fish while it bakes. The skin of fish is not permeable, so the fish will not taste extra salty as a result of this method; if the skin were permeable, then all fish would taste salty, because fish swim in salt water their entire lives—but that's not the case.

You want the salt crust to have plenty of flavor, so you're going to make the salt aromatic. Starting with coarse salt, add some orange zest and lemon zest to it. Then, add some crushed star anise and ground fennel. Add some fine salt as well. Make sure that all of the spices are well mixed and that the lemon zest and orange zest are broken up.

You want the crust to form on the outside of the fish, and some beaten egg white is going to hold it all together. Add egg white to your mixture and stir. You want to use just enough egg white to moisten the salt. If you use too much egg white, then it will run out of the crust and you'll have fried egg all around the outside of the fish.

In a pan, make a bed of salt, which will protect the fish from the bottom of the pan. Then, transfer the fish to the pan. Mound the salt mixture on top of the

fish, forming a crust, but leave the head and tail exposed. Pat the crust on the outside of the fish to smooth it out.

Bake the fish in the oven at 425 degrees. How do you determine doneness when the fish is buried deep inside a crust of salt? The thickest part of the meat will be right behind the collar, and if you have a thermometer, you can pierce the shell of salt and take the temperature in that region of the fish. You want to take the fish out of the oven at about 130 degrees, with the understanding that the salt crust will continue to cook the fish and bring it all the way up to 145 or 150 degrees, which is where you want to eat it.

After taking the fish out of the oven, you have to crack through the salt crust. Using a knife, crack the crust right around the base of where you think the fish begins, both in the front and back of the fish. Then, using a fork, you should be able to peel the salt crust and skin off the fish. Cut through the meat and ease the fish off the bone by lifting the spine up and away from the fish. Remove everything that was stuffed into the belly of the fish.

You might be inclined to squeeze some lemon on top of the fish, but it really just needs a simple sauce: extra-virgin olive oil. When serving this fish, bring some olive oil to the table, and anoint the fish with oil in front of your guests. The oil makes the fish taste fresher, livelier, and richer.

Calabrian Tomato Soup

Ingredients

Yield: 6 portions

- ½ cup extra-virgin olive oil
- 1 ½ lbs ripe tomatoes, cored and chopped
- 6 parsley branches
- 2 garlic cloves
- 1–2 Fresno chiles, or ½–¾ tsp chile flakes
- 1 pt chicken stock
- 6 day-old bread slices, rustic
- 2 oz Parmesan
- salt and pepper, to taste

To make a simple tomato soup that is a great vehicle for exploring all the different flavors of olive oil, you need some tomatoes, garlic, parsley, and pepper flakes.

Start by cutting up the tomatoes and chopping the garlic and parsley. In a pot, combine all of the ingredients and stew them together very briefly. Then, add chicken stock and let it simmer. You want to cook it until the tomatoes just begin to collapse and until the garlic is soft. Then, you're going to put it through a food mill to remove all the seeds, skins, and stems.

Once everything that you don't want in your finished soup is removed, pour the liquid back into the same pot. At this point, taste the soup to determine how it needs to be seasoned with salt and pepper. Ripe tomatoes, especially,

demand a lot of salt, so you might need to add a little more than you normally would. If you decide that your soup is too thick, you can always add some water or stock to it to thin it out. Then, bring it back up to a simmer so that it's hot when you serve it.

Serve this soup over grilled bread. And just so that there's a lot of nooks and crannies for the soup to be absorbed into, grill the bread and then break it up into pieces. Sprinkle some cheese on top of the soup, and it's ready to be served.

This simple tomato soup can be elevated by olive oil. You might choose one that has a little bit of a tomato leaf flavor, which will complement what you taste in the soup. But don't go out looking for a specific oil. This is a great excuse to explore a lot of different oils. You could serve the soup along with three oils on the table that you could explore and add to the soup.

Budino (Chocolate Custard)

Ingredients

Yield: 10–12 portions

- 8.5 oz bittersweet chocolate
- ½ cup whole milk
- 2 cups cream
- ½ cup sugar
- 7 egg yolks
- ¼ oz Maldon salt
- 3 oz extra-virgin olive oil
- 3 oz orange marmalade, optional

To enjoy olive oil in a dessert seems almost unreasonable, but it actually tastes great. To try the combination of a chocolate dessert with olive oil, make a quick chocolate custard, or *budino*.

Start by warming some cream and milk in a pan. In a bowl, whip some egg yolks with a little bit of sugar. When you add sugar to egg yolks, make sure you don't let the sugar just sit in contact with the egg yolks for too long, because they will burn, and you'll end up with small flecks of hard egg yolk that will never dissolve. Whip the egg yolks and sugar until you get a lighter consistency so that you know the mixture is uniform.

Next, melt some chocolate. You can melt chocolate in the microwave, but you can also just put it over warm water in a bowl and let it melt gently. You don't want to burn it. For this recipe, the darker the chocolate, the better, within reason. Use about 60 to 70 percent cocoa solids.

Add the melted chocolate to the whipped egg yolk mixture and stir it all together. Then, add the warm cream to the chocolate mixture. Add the cream in a few different parts, which will allow the mixture to get thin incrementally.

You're going to bake this custard in a water bath, which will allow the heat of the oven to be tempered. Eggs are kind of temperamental. Even if you put the custard into an oven at 325 degrees, the water that surrounds it will keep the temperature down below boiling. The egg yolks will sct, and the custard will become a semisolid.

Pour the custard into an ovenproof dish inside of a second dish that is slightly larger. Pour hot water about halfway up the side of the second dish. Then, carefully put the dishes into the oven. Bake for about 15 minutes at 325 degrees.

Top the custard with some orange marmalade, if desired. Finish the custard with a strong, vibrant olive oil, which will go well with the full-flavored chocolate, and a good-quality salt.

Paella—The Landscape of Spain in a Pan

Lesson 6

Many people think of paella as the national dish of Spain. Some people even consider paella the landscape of Spain in a pan. In fact, paella is named for the pan that it is cooked in. In this lesson, you will learn how to make paella—a simple main dish that is cooked all in one pan. You will also learn how to make an appetizer of marinated olives and a simple side salad called *escalivada*.

Warm Olives in Thyme and Orange Marinade

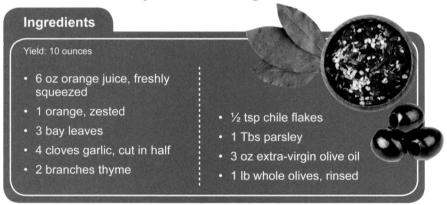

Ingredients

Yield: 10 ounces

- 6 oz orange juice, freshly squeezed
- 1 orange, zested
- 3 bay leaves
- 4 cloves garlic, cut in half
- 2 branches thyme

- ½ tsp chile flakes
- 1 Tbs parsley
- 3 oz extra-virgin olive oil
- 1 lb whole olives, rinsed

To make the marinade for this appetizer, reduce some orange juice down to a syrup in a pan. Then, add some bay leaves, garlic, thyme, and pepper flakes (if desired). Also add the zest of an orange so that it tastes more like an orange than just a reduced orange juice.

Add some olives, along with some olive oil, to the marinade in the pan, tossing them to warm them slightly. Warming olives, especially when they're marinated, brings out a tremendous amount of flavor. Then, add some parsley and serve warm.

You can marinate the olives for a few weeks, keeping them in the refrigerator until you want to serve them. If you do this, first bring the olives to room temperature before putting them in a sauté pan and heating them until they sizzle.

Serve with a glass of sherry as a great way to start a meal.

Escalivada Catalana (Roasted Eggplant, Peppers, Onions, and Tomatoes, Catalan-style)

Ingredients

Yield: 4 portions

- 1 eggplant, medium
- 1 Spanish onion, large
- 1 red bell pepper
- 3 ripe tomatoes, large

- ¼ cup extra-virgin olive oil (plus extra for coating the vegetables)
- ½ Tbs sherry vinegar
- salt, to taste
- white pepper, to taste

Escalivada is a roasted vegetable salad that contains eggplant, peppers, onions, and tomatoes. To make this salad, toss these vegetables in olive oil and bake them in the oven at about 400 degrees until they are slightly charred, caramelized, and very tender.

Once the vegetables are removed from the oven, first capture the liquid that comes off of the vegetables. Put it into a bowl and set aside.

Then, once the vegetables have cooled off, remove their skins. Cut the skin of the eggplant open and spread it out. If the eggplant has a lot of seeds, pull some of them out and discard them. Then, with a fork, shred the flesh of the eggplant and separate it from the skin. The blackened skin of the pepper should be easy to peel off. Then, cut the peppers into strips. Next, peel the onions and cut them into slices, after removing the root and stem ends. Finally, peel the skin off the tomatoes, chopping them into a course puree.

Arrange the vegetables on a plate, paying attention to color. Season the vegetables with salt and pepper. To the roasting liquid you put in a bowl, add some sherry vinegar and olive oil, and then stir. Spoon the liquid mixture over the vegetables as a dressing. Just to brighten it up, add some chopped parsley, if desired. This salad can sit for about an hour before your meal is ready to go.

Paella Valenciana

Ingredients

Yield: 6 portions

- 6 cups chicken stock (might need extra to cook the rice)
- 1 pinch saffron
- salt, to taste
- 1 lb chicken thigh, bone out, diced
- ½ lb Spanish chorizo
- ⅓ cup olive oil
- ¾ cup red bell pepper, diced small
- ¾ cup green bell pepper, medium dice

- ½ cup Spanish onion, medium dice
- 1 Tbs garlic, minced
- 3 cups short-grain Spanish rice (*bomba*)
- 4 mussels
- 4 clams
- 4 shrimp
- 1 cup green peas
- 1 lemon, juiced
- 1 lemon, cut into wedges

Despite all of the variety that you can find, keep in mind that paella is first and foremost a rice dish and that all of the other garnishes are included just to add flavor to the rice. Don't focus on all of the different things that can be added to the rice; pay attention to the rice itself.

Paella is a traditional Spanish dish. To prepare for paella, cook some vegetables, including onions, peppers, and garlic, for about an hour to an hour and a half in olive oil. Season with salt. This is called *sofrito*, and it is made in large batches and is considered to be a staple in Spanish kitchens.

To make paella, start by browning some deboned and diced chicken thighs in a pan. Then, add some chorizo, a Spanish sausage that is flavored with paprika. Let it cook and sizzle. The fat will render out.

Add the *sofrito* to the paella pan. Then, add rice, coating it with the flavorful fat that's in the bottom of the pan. Next, introduce

Types of Paella

There are many different types of paella. Some people like to eat paella that has pork chops in it, while others like paella with lobster tails. Possibly the first and oldest version of paella was made with rabbit and snails. Some paellas have mint-scented lamb meatballs that flavor the rice. Other paellas are made with wild mushrooms and grilled quail. A traditional paella contains chorizo, chicken, and seafood (mussels, clams, and shrimp).

chicken stock steeped with saffron. Taste the stock to make sure that it is properly seasoned. You want a stock that will add flavor to this preparation. Turn down the heat until the contents of the pan are simmering. Make sure to have extra stock on hand in case your rice is not quite done and needs more liquid.

The rice in this paella is called *bomba* rice, which is a Spanish short-grain rice. Short-grain rice tends to cook very sticky and starchy, which will give body to the dish. *Bomba* is distinctive because it holds its shape very well throughout cooking.

Don't stir the rice constantly, because if you do, the paella will become akin to risotto, which is not what you want. Instead of stirring, just give the pan a little shake. You want all of the rice to be submerged in the cooking liquid. Use a spoon to make sure there isn't any rice stuck to the pan, especially to the bottom of the middle of the pan.

Cook the paella for about 25 minutes. As the liquid begins to be absorbed, reduce the heat a little. When it's cooked about halfway—after about 10 to 12 minutes—introduce some ingredients that don't need to cook for the entire time: fresh peas (or green beans), clams, mussels, and shrimp. Press the peas into the liquid so that they can cook.

Before you cook the shellfish, examine each for quality. If you notice that a clam or mussel is gapped open, squeeze it, and if it closes up tight, that tells you that the shellfish is still alive. If, on the other hand, it's gapped open and stays open when you squeeze it, this indicates that the shellfish has already died, and it can be dangerous to eat. Discard shellfish like this.

Make sure that the shellfish are added to the pan with the seam, or hinge, down so that their shells can open as they cook. When the shellfish open, they lend

Short-, Medium-, and Long-Grain Rice

Arborio rice, which is used to make risotto, is a short-grain rice. The grains of this rice are no more than two times as long as they are wide. This type of rice has a lot of starch, and the Italians capitalize on that starchiness by stirring it constantly while it's cooking, creating a creamy gravy. Likewise, the Japanese use short-grain rice for sushi, because they want the rice to stick together into fingers, or logs.

Medium-grain rice, such as jasmine rice, is about three times as long as it is wide. When this type of rice is cooked, it is less sticky than short-grain rice. The eastern Mediterranean—Turkey, specifically—is famous for pilaf. The pilaf method, which involves parching the rice in a pan of hot fat, guarantees that the rice doesn't clump together.

Long-grain rice is about five times as long as it is wide. When it is cooked, it becomes very fluffy. In general, Americans like to use long-grain rice.

It is important to choose the right rice for the dish you are making.

more liquid to the broth. Of the three types of shellfish, the clams take longer than the other two to cook, so you should add those to the pan first. Then, add the mussels. As the clams and mussels cook, their shells will protect them from the heat of the rice below. Finally, add the shrimp, making sure to flip them over at some point so that their second side has access to the heat.

As the paella cooks, the rice absorbs the liquid. To monitor the progress of the rice, periodically taste it. Specifically, you can bite into a single grain or two of rice, and if you see a chalky core, that is indicative of rice that hasn't fully cooked yet.

Once the rice is cooked, turn up the heat a little higher, because it's desirable for the rice to get dry on the bottom of the pan and then begin to cling to the pan and brown just a little bit, forming a crust on the bottom of the pan. Watch the pan carefully, because you don't want the paella to burn. It should be golden and moist, but as you move the pan back and forth, the rice should start to stick to the bottom of the pan, which means that the crust is forming.

Once all the shellfish have opened and the shrimp are fully cooked, put the finishing touches on the paella. Chop some parsley, and sprinkle some on top. Garnish with slices of lemon, tucking them in around the edges of the paella, and squeeze some lemon juice on top.

White wine is typically paired with paella, but if you prefer red wine, choose a lighter, fruitier red. A good compromise would be a rosé.

A Spanish Tradition— Tapas and Sherry

Lesson 7

In this lesson, you will learn about the small-dish tradition of Spain known as tapas. Specifically, you will learn how to make five different tapas that you can put together to create your own tapas spread. Tapas can be composed of grilled food, stewed food, or even raw food, along with olives, cheese, or almonds. All of these ingredients make up a class of small dishes that often is enjoyed separate from a meal. Traditionally, tapas are served with a glass of sherry, which is made in Spain.

Bartender's Chorizo

Ingredients

Yield: 6 portions

- 3 Spanish chorizo
- 1 Tbs olive oil
- ⅓ cup brandy

- 4 oz goat cheese, aged
- 1 small baguette

To make bartender's chorizo, start with some chorizo, which are pork sausages from Spain that are flavored with smoky paprika. Heat them up in a pan with olive oil until they are browned.

Sherry

Sherry, which is a strong wine that is made in Spain, is often served with tapas instead of as a table wine. Aperitif sherries are consumed before a meal, with tapas, because they are too strong to enjoy with a meal. Dessert sherries are consumed after a meal.

Aperitif Sherries

Fino is a dry sherry that is a great crisp wine to enjoy with salty ingredients like olives and salted almonds, or maybe with grilled, poached, or marinated seafood.

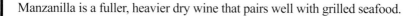

Manzanilla is a fuller, heavier dry wine that pairs well with grilled seafood.

Amontillado is not quite as dry or sharp as fino and Manzanilla. Its sweetness and nuttiness go well with Marcona almonds, for example. This type of rounder, softer sherry is enjoyed with heavier foods, such as bartender's chorizo.

Oloroso is aged for extra time, so it is sweeter and nuttier in flavor. This wine can be enjoyed with something rich like pâté.

Palo cortado is a rare sherry that tastes like a mixture between a fino and an amontillado. It has the bright acidity and crispness of a fino with the nuttiness of an amontillado. It's a light, refreshing wine.

Dessert Sherries

Cream sherry is a very sweet and nutty wine that is a delightful way to end a meal.

Pedro Ximénez is a very sweet and syrupy dessert wine.

When this dish gets ordered in a tapas bar, it is served in a special dish called an *asador*. What makes this dish distinctive is that the sausages are suspended above the *cazuela* below by slings that go from one side to the other. The chorizo comes out hot to the bar, and the bartender pours brandy over the sausages and then the brandy, which is captured in the *cazuela* below the sausages, is set on fire. The sausages warm over the fire of the brandy that is burning below. Little by little, the sausages crisp up and warm.

Serve with goat cheese and sliced baguette.

Tortilla Española (Spanish Potato and Egg Tapas)

Ingredients

Yield: 6–8 portions

- ¾ cup extra-virgin olive oil
- 4 potatoes, cut into ⅛-inch slices

- 1 onion, thinly sliced
- 2 tsp salt
- 5 eggs

A Spanish tortilla—unlike a Mexican tortilla, which involves a corn or wheat tortilla—is like an omelet that hasn't been folded over (a flat omelet). It starts with potatoes that have been sliced very thin. Russet potatoes are preferable. Cook the potatoes in a hot pan with olive oil.

Be careful that you don't cook the potatoes too aggressively or too quickly. You want them to cook, but you don't want them to cook until they're brown and crispy. You're going to add eggs to the pan, and you want the eggs to absorb into the potatoes, which won't happen if there's a crust on the outside of the potatoes. You also want the flavor of the olive oil to be absorbed into the potatoes, and that won't happen if they fry to a crisp crust on the outside.

Continue to cook the potatoes over a moderate heat, periodically scraping them off the bottom of the pan. If the potatoes stick to the pan, it's probably because the pan is not hot enough. After about four or five minutes of cooking the potatoes, add some onions to the pan and cook them for another four or five minutes. Once the potatoes are tender and the onions are translucent, strain the potatoes and onions out of the oil. Put some of this oil aside; it will be used in a pan to cook the Spanish tortilla.

Let the potatoes cool a little bit, because if you combine the potatoes and eggs while the potatoes are still hot, the eggs will immediately cook on the outside of the potatoes. Once the potato mixture is sufficiently cool, add it to the eggs. You want to use just enough eggs to bind the potatoes without having a lot of extra egg. Season the potatoes and eggs with some salt, just as though you were making scrambled eggs for breakfast.

To make the tortilla, heat a pan on the stove with the oil you saved from the potatoes and onions. Once the oil is hot, add the potatoes and eggs all at once. Once the tortilla starts to firm up and move independent of the pan, turn down the heat a little. You want a crust to form on the bottom of the tortilla that is forming in the pan; periodically check the bottom to monitor how it's browning.

After about four minutes, check the bottom of the mixture to see if it's ready to be flipped onto its other side. You should see a golden crust on the bottom, and there shouldn't be a lot of liquid egg left in the pan. At this point, put a lid or large plate on top of the pan, and flip the pan over so that the tortilla ends up on the lid or plate. Then, with the help of a spatula, slide the tortilla back into the pan so that the uncooked side is making contact with the pan.

Before the liquid egg on the bottom side cooks, use a spatula to shape the tortilla, tucking the edges underneath to make it look more uniform. After about two minutes, the second side of the tortilla should be fully cooked, and you can pull it off the heat and slide it onto a plate.

Serve the tortilla with garlic mayonnaise. Garnish with parsley, if desired. Cut the tortilla into about six to eight small slices so that several people can enjoy it.

This recipe is the most basic recipe for a Spanish tortilla. In addition to the potatoes and onions, you can add ingredients such as ham, salt cod, sautéed mushrooms, or spinach. Be creative.

Stuffed Olives

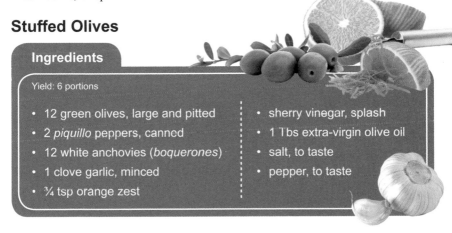

Ingredients

Yield: 6 portions

- 12 green olives, large and pitted
- 2 *piquillo* peppers, canned
- 12 white anchovies (*boquerones*)
- 1 clove garlic, minced
- ¾ tsp orange zest
- sherry vinegar, splash
- 1 Tbs extra-virgin olive oil
- salt, to taste
- pepper, to taste

To make this simple tapa, start with some pitted green olives. Cut them open— but not all the way through—at the top. Insert a white anchovy that has been cured and then soaked in olive oil and white wine vinegar. On top of the white anchovy, put some roasted pepper. Of course, you can decide what you want to stuff the olives with. Common ingredients include garlic, jalapeños, blue cheese, or pimento cheese.

Next, make a simple dressing to go on top of the stuffed olives. Put some garlic in a bowl with some orange zest, sherry vinegar, olive oil, salt, and pepper. The olives, anchovies, and roasted peppers all taste great on their own, so you don't need to add too much dressing to the stuffed olives. Taste the dressing to make sure you're happy with the flavor, and then spoon it on top of the stuffed olives.

Padrón Peppers

Ingredients

Yield: 6 portions

- 1 lb padrón peppers
- 2 Tbs olive oil

- ½ lemon, juiced
- ½ tsp salt

When padrón peppers mature, they become spicy, but if they are harvested when they're small, they won't be too spicy. They are sometimes called roulette peppers, because every so often, you'll get a spicy one.

To make a tapa with padrón peppers, start by sautéing them in a very hot pan with olive oil to blister the outsides and to soften the flesh. Don't introduce the peppers until the oil is very hot. You might even wait for the first wisp or two of gray smoke to come off the pan. Once you add the padrón peppers, turn the heat down a little. You can use tongs to toss the peppers around in the pan periodically so that they don't burn.

After only about a minute or less, the skin of the peppers will blister and blacken. Once about 50 to 70 percent of the surface of each pepper is blistered, then they are ready to be served.

Put the peppers onto a plate. As a dressing, squeeze some lemon juice on top of the peppers, along with some good-quality sea salt. Don't be shy with the salt; these peppers taste better if they're aggressively seasoned.

Champiñones al Ajillo (Mushrooms in Garlic Sauce)

Ingredients

Yield: 12 portions

- ⅓ cup Spanish extra-virgin olive oil
- 1 lb mushrooms, stems trimmed, cleaned, cut into ¼-inch-thick slices or left whole if very small
- 8 garlic cloves, peeled, thinly sliced

- ¼ cup dry (fino) Spanish sherry
- ½ tsp crushed red pepper
- salt, to taste
- ground black pepper, to taste
- 2 branches thyme

To make this dish, start with some mushrooms. If you want to use white button mushrooms, break the stems off. Instead, if you want to use white trumpet mushrooms, cut them in half and score the flesh. Next, sauté the mushrooms in some olive oil in a pan on the heat. Mushrooms tend to be thirsty, so they tend to like a lot of oil. If you are using white trumpet mushrooms, lay their big, flat side down in the pan.

Cook the mushrooms until they are brown and tender. While they're beginning to brown, if you discover that the mushrooms are drinking more oil than you're comfortable adding, you can introduce a little water to the pan instead. The water begins to break down the cell structure of the mushroom, which is kind of like a sponge, causing it to release some of the oil that it has absorbed.

Season the mushrooms with salt, ground black pepper, crushed red pepper flakes, thyme, and sliced garlic. Monitor the cooking of the mushrooms to make sure that none of these ingredients burn. When you notice the garlic beginning to turn golden, you can cool down the pan by adding some water. The introduction of this liquid to the pan will allow the ingredients to continue cooking without burning.

Once the garlic turns a golden color, add some Manzanilla sherry to the pan to deglaze it. Cook the liquid down until its consistency becomes similar to that of a sauce. In other words, it shouldn't be very wet or soupy. Before serving, taste the sauce and adjust seasoning as needed.

Tunisia—The Home of *Harissa*

Lesson 8

In this lesson, we will travel to Tunisia, which is on the North African coastline. Its central location in the Mediterranean and deep harbors has made it attractive to seafarers for many years. Traditionally, most of the meals—in Tunisia or any other of the North African countries—begin with small dishes known as mezes. In this lesson, you will learn three different salads that are simple and easy to prepare, along with two other dishes that are staples in Tunisia.

Zucchini with *Chermoula*

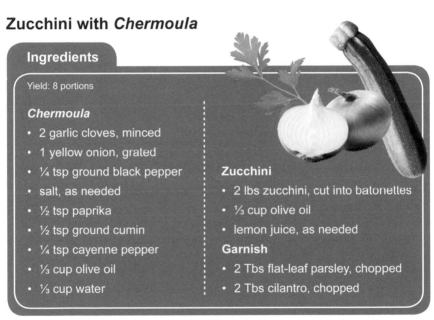

Ingredients

Yield: 8 portions

Chermoula
- 2 garlic cloves, minced
- 1 yellow onion, grated
- ¼ tsp ground black pepper
- salt, as needed
- ½ tsp paprika
- ½ tsp ground cumin
- ¼ tsp cayenne pepper
- ⅓ cup olive oil
- ⅓ cup water

Zucchini
- 2 lbs zucchini, cut into batonettes
- ⅓ cup olive oil
- lemon juice, as needed

Garnish
- 2 Tbs flat-leaf parsley, chopped
- 2 Tbs cilantro, chopped

Chermoula is a pervasive condiment in both Tunisia and Morocco. To make zucchini with *chermoula*, start by cutting some zucchini in half, and then into quarters. To help them cook evenly but also make them look attractive, cut the zucchini pieces into batonettes, which involves cutting them into rectangular shapes. In a hot pan, sauté the zucchini in some olive oil.

While the zucchini is browning, prepare the dressing. Gather the cilantro and parsley into a tight bundle, and then chop through them once, making the herbs uniformly fine. Season with salt and pepper.

Once you see the first signs of browning on the zucchini, reduce the heat and add some finely chopped onion. Once the onion turns translucent, add some garlic. Once the garlic is aromatic, add the spices: cumin, paprika, and cayenne. In a hot pan, spices will burn very quickly, so turn the heat down a little and add some water to the pan to stop the intense heat. In addition to cooling the pan, the water will help the zucchini cook to tenderness.

Then, add the chopped herbs and turn the heat off. Add some lemon juice, and if it looks a little dry, add a drop or two of olive oil.

Serve this salad at room temperature.

Carrot Salad with *Harissa*, Feta, and Olives

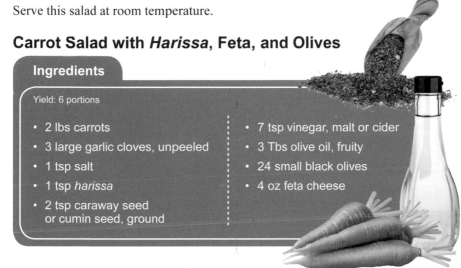

Ingredients

Yield: 6 portions

- 2 lbs carrots
- 3 large garlic cloves, unpeeled
- 1 tsp salt
- 1 tsp *harissa*
- 2 tsp caraway seed or cumin seed, ground

- 7 tsp vinegar, malt or cider
- 3 Tbs olive oil, fruity
- 24 small black olives
- 4 oz feta cheese

To make this salad, start by cooking some carrots in boiling, salted water with a clove or two of garlic. Once the carrots are tender, strain them from the water and crush them with the back of a fork— or a potato masher, if you have one—to create a rough mash of carrots (not a puree).

Make a dressing for the carrots, starting with oil and vinegar (lemon juice can be used as an alternative to vinegar). Then, add caraway or cumin, salt, and *harissa*, which is a chile paste from Tunisia. It is primarily dried chiles that are rehydrated and pureed, but it also contains garlic, coriander seed, and caraway. *Harissa* is a flavoring agent, not a condiment, so be careful not to use too much because it can be spicy.

To tie the dressing together, pour some of the cooking liquid used to boil the carrots over the carrot salad. Stir the ingredients of the salad, and as toppings, add black olives and sprinkle some crumbled feta cheese on top of the salad. Taste it to make sure you are happy with the flavor before serving.

Fennel Salad with Preserved Lemon and Garlic

Ingredients

Yield: 6 portions

- 2–3 large fennel bulbs, trimmed
- ¼ preserved lemon
- 2 garlic cloves, minced
- 2–3 Tbs lemon juice
- 3 Tbs extra-virgin olive oil

- 1 tsp salt
- ¼ tsp ground black pepper
- ¼ cup cilantro leaves

This is a salad of shaved fennel that is flavored with preserved lemon. Using a knife—or a mandoline, if you have one—shave some fennel very thin and put it in a bowl.

To the fennel, add some preserved lemon. Lemons are a seasonal crop, so preserving them in salt makes them available the whole year. Preserved lemon has been preserved in salt, which allows you to push the flesh of the lemon from the rind very easily. Cut the rind of the lemon very thin, because it's salty, and add it to the salad. Squeeze the meat of the lemon, and add some of the liquid to the salad.

Because preserved lemon contains a lot of salt, only add a little salt to the salad, along with some pepper. Then, chop up some cilantro and add that as well. Make some garlic into a paste and add it to the bowl.

Dress the salad with olive oil and lemon juice. Because the fennel is raw, this salad would benefit from sitting for about an hour before serving so that the salt could start to soften the crisp fennel and make it more tender.

Brik de Maman

Brik is a savory pastry that can be considered the national pastry of Tunisia. To make this dish, rice some cooked potato into a bowl. To the potato, add canned tuna that was packed in olive oil, finely diced onions, chopped capers, coarsely chopped parsley, and *harissa*. Stir everything together. Taste this potato filling to make sure that you're happy with the flavor. Add a little bit of lemon and salt. Bind the filling with some egg. There shouldn't be any liquid egg that can run out.

This is a pretty typical *brik* filling, but you'll see esoteric versions of this pastry that have fillings that include lamb brain, anchovies, and other vegetables. It's not uncommon for these fillings to contain egg.

The pastry that you're going to wrap this filling in is *brik* pastry. It is a very thin pastry that is made by dabbing a very moist dough on the back of a hot pan and letting the dough stick to it. When the dough is cooked, it is peeled away from the pan. You can buy it frozen, and unlike phyllo dough, which can be temperamental, *brik* is pretty forgiving.

Cut a piece of the *brik* pastry in half and add some of the potato filling to the center of the pastry. Then, using a pastry brush (if you have one), moisten the

edges of the pastry with water so that it sticks to itself. Fold the edges of the pastry over about three or four times. Then, repeat with the other half of the pastry.

Deep-fry the stuffed pastries in a pan or fryer with hot oil that is about 370 degrees. Lower the pastries into the hot fat, laying them away from yourself in order to avoid the splash of hot oil burning your skin.

Once the pastries turn a golden color, drain any excess oil from them, first over the pan and then on an absorbent towel. They are best served right from the fryer or pan. Like a lot of fried food, *brik* benefit from some lemon squeezed over them.

Always remember to turn the heat off when you're done cooking with oil. Never walk away and leave it unattended.

Tagine Ricotta (Tunisian Cheese and Egg *Tagine*)

Ingredients

Yield: 6 portions

- 4 cardamom seeds, removed from pods
- 4 cloves
- 1 tsp ground ginger
- 1 tsp cumin seeds
- 1 tsp ground cinnamon
- 1 tsp coriander seeds
- ½ tsp black peppercorns
- 3 garlic cloves, finely minced
- ¾ lb lamb, ground
- ¼ cup extra-virgin olive oil

- ½ cup onion, minced
- 3–4 Tbs ground cumin
- 1 tsp saffron
- salt, to taste
- ground black pepper, to taste
- 6 eggs, beaten
- ¼ lb Gruyère cheese, grated
- 2 eggs, hard-boiled, finely chopped
- 1 lb ricotta cheese

If you order a *tagine* in Tunisia, it comes out in a shallow ovenproof dish with no lid, and the contents are bound with egg and cheese. On the other hand, if you order a *tagine* in Morocco, it is a liquid stew either with fish, vegetables, or maybe lamb.

To make a Tunisian *tagine*, start by sautéing some onions in a hot pan with oil. Once the onions become translucent, add some ground lamb seasoned with a selection of exotic spices, including cardamom, cloves, ginger, cumin, cinnamon, coriander, and black pepper. If you want this preparation to be richer, you can add some saffron as well. Then, season the meat with salt. Once the lamb is browned, turn the heat off and let the lamb cool.

Put just enough oil in a pan to coat it so that nothing sticks. Mix together some egg and some Gruyère cheese. The egg will bind the *tagine* together. Season with salt and pepper.

Add a third of the eggs and cheese to the bottom of a shallow ovenproof dish. Once that cooks, it will create a crust. Then, add about half of the lamb and spread it around. On top of that, add some ricotta cheese. Press some chopped hard-boiled eggs into the mixture.

Next, add another third of the egg custard and spread it around. Then, add the rest of the lamb, chopped hard-boiled eggs, and ricotta cheese, in that order. Season with salt and pepper. Finish with the remaining third of the egg and cheese, spreading it evenly over the top.

Bake the *tagine* in a preheated oven at about 375 degrees for about 30 minutes. You want to make sure that the egg is fully cooked. Once the *tagine* becomes firm and the cheese becomes brown on the top, remove it from the oven. Garnish with chopped parsley and serve while it's still warm from the oven.

Technique and Polish—
Mastering Moroccan Food
Lesson 9

In this lesson, we will spend some time in Morocco. Tunisia and Morocco are almost neighbors to one another, and there are many similarities in their cuisines. For example, both Morocco and Tunisia use sweet spices. But there are also some striking differences. Tunisian food seems simpler, more like the food you might eat at home, while Moroccan food is more refined and polished. In this lesson, you will see these differences as you learn how to cook *bisteeya* and a seven-vegetable couscous.

Bisteeya (Chicken-Filled Pastry)

Ingredients

Yield: 10 portions

- ½ cup extra-virgin olive oil, plus as needed for assembly
- 2 lbs chicken thigh meat
- salt, to taste
- ground black pepper, to taste
- 2 cups onions, diced small
- 2 tsp ginger, minced
- ½ tsp ground mace
- ½ tsp nutmeg, freshly grated
- ¼ tsp ground cloves
- 1 ½ tsp ground cinnamon, plus as needed for topping

- chicken stock, as needed
- ¼ cup butter
- ⅓ cup cilantro, chopped
- ⅓ cup flat-leaf parsley, chopped
- ½ tsp saffron
- ¼ cup brown sugar
- 8 eggs, lightly beaten
- ½ lb almonds, toasted, coarsely chopped
- 2 lbs phyllo dough
- powdered sugar, as needed

Bisteeya ("pigeon pie") is a savory pastry that was once made with squab, or pigeon. Instead, this recipe uses chicken.

Start by browning some chicken thighs in a pan with oil. Then, add onions and spices, including cinnamon, cloves, nutmeg, mace, and ginger. Once the onions are tender and the spices are aromatic, add some chicken stock and braise the chicken for about 45 minutes to an hour. Once the chicken is very

tender, remove it from the pan, leaving behind the braising liquid, which is the heart and soul of a braised dish. Allow the chicken to cool off.

Once the braising liquid is free of chicken, bring it up to a boil and reduce it until it's very concentrated. As it's reducing, add some saffron, which should be added late in the cooking so that it doesn't lose its aroma. Then, add some brown sugar. This is a savory dish, but it also has overtones of sweetness—a trait that is very common in Moroccan food.

While the liquid in the pan is reducing, whip some eggs. Once the liquid is reduced to a glaze, taste it to make sure that it's properly seasoned with salt and pepper, and adjust accordingly. Specifically, make sure that there's enough salt to balance the sweetness of the sugar. Add the reduced braising liquid to the beaten eggs and scramble them in a hot pan. Once the eggs are scrambled, take them off the heat. To brighten it up, stir in some parsley and cilantro.

Once the chicken is cooled, use a fork to pull it apart and shred it. Discard anything objectionable you find along the way, such as gristle, skin, or bones. It is easier to do this when the chicken is cool, so put it in the refrigerator if you need to cool it down quickly.

To build a *bisteeya*, use phyllo pastry, which is a very thin pastry that you can buy frozen. Brush a small ovenproof pan with melted butter, or olive oil if you'd prefer. Then, layer the phyllo pastry in the pan one piece at a time, with the edges of the pastry hanging over the edge of the pan, brushing each layer with butter before adding the next one. Repeat this process until you have laid 10 leaves of pastry into the pan as a base.

Any excess butter will drain off, so don't worry about using too much, especially because you don't want the phyllo to dry out. You have to be able to fold it up and over a filling, and it will dry out if it sits out too long. The butter helps keep it moist.

Next, add the filling, starting with the shredded chicken, along with any extra herbs that you want to add. Then, put the eggs that were cooked with the braising liquid on top of the chicken. Top the eggs with toasted almonds. Finally, bring the hanging dough over the top of the filling, containing the filling within the dough.

Then, build the top of the pastry by laying about five more leaves of dough on top of the dough you folded over. Moisten the edges of the dough so that they don't dry out. If you have a similar-sized pan, the easiest way to finish this is to put another pan on top of the pastry, turn the whole thing over, and bring the overhanging dough up and over the top of the pastry.

Bake the pastry in the oven at about 375 degrees for about 10 minutes, until it is browned on the surface. Remember that all of the filling is completely cooked already, so you're only interested in browning the pastry. Once the top is browned, flip the pastry over so that the other side has a chance to brown. Leave it on its second side for another 10 or 15 minutes, until both sides are a deep golden color.

After removing the pastry from the oven, get rid of any excess butter by dabbing it with a paper towel. Finish the pastry in a traditional way, by dusting it with powdered sugar and striping it with cinnamon. Serve while it's still hot.

Seven-Vegetable Couscous

Ingredients

Yield: 6 servings

- 2 onions, sliced
- 4 Tbs clarified butter
- 3 tomatoes, peeled and chopped
- 2 tsp cinnamon
- ¾ tsp ginger
- 3 pinches saffron
- ½ tsp turmeric
- 6 cups vegetable or chicken stock
- 3 carrots, cut into large chunks
- 1 cup chickpeas, cooked
- 3 zucchini, halved
- 2 cups pumpkin or other hard squash, cut into fingers ¾ inch by ¾ inch by 3 inch

- 3 turnips, peeled and cut into sixths
- 1 red pepper cut into sixths
- 1 green pepper cut into sixths
- ½ preserved lemon, peel only, sliced thin
- salt, to taste
- ground black pepper, to taste
- ⅓ cup cilantro, chopped
- 2 Tbs parsley, chopped
- 1 lb couscous, cooked, with black raisins and slivered almonds

To make this dish, start by adding some butter to a hot pan. As the butter melts, add sliced onions. As the onions begin to turn translucent, add some spices, including cinnamon, ginger, turmeric, and saffron (which has been soaked in warm water to get the color and flavor out of it). Then, add some chopped tomatoes (canned tomatoes are fine).

Start the process of seasoning the vegetables with salt and pepper, but also revisit the seasoning many times while this dish cooks. Taste this dish as it cooks to see how it develops. Next, add chicken stock, or vegetable stock if you prefer to make this a vegetarian dish. If you're not making this as a vegetarian dish, you can also add lamb or chicken to this stew.

As the stew comes up to a boil, add five more vegetables to the two that are already in the pan (onions and tomatoes) to satisfy the seven-vegetable recipe. The remaining vegetables are carrots, turnips, zucchini,

Lucky Number Seven

The significance of seven vegetables in the seven-vegetable couscous is interesting. In Morocco, the number seven is considered to be auspicious. So, while there are seven specific vegetables in this recipe, you could choose different vegetables. As long as you stick to seven, the luck will be with you.

butternut squash (or pumpkin), and peppers. Peppers cook quickly, but carrots and turnips take longer, so add the carrots and turnips earlier in the cooking process than the peppers. Also add cooked chickpeas before putting a lid on the pan, reducing the heat, and letting it simmer for about 15 or 20 minutes.

Once most of the vegetables are tender, add chopped cilantro and chopped parsley to the stew. Then, add some preserved lemon. Because the lemon has been preserved in a salt brine, you can easily pull the meat of the lemon right off of the rind. Slice the rind very thin, because it tends to be very salty.

Once the broth starts to take on a body, because of the starch making its way out of all the various vegetables, taste the broth to determine whether it needs more flavor. To add flavor, add extra cinnamon or ginger, for example. Once you are satisfied with the flavor of the broth and the vegetables are very tender, turn off the burner.

You're going to serve this stew with couscous, which is a pasta. You're going to cook it in the traditional Moroccan way, instead of according to the directions on the package.

Wash the couscous in abundant water (three times as much water as couscous) and then drain it. Allow it to rehydrate and rub any lumps out of it. Then, mound it in a *couscousière* (a pot designed specifically for making couscous) and steam it for 20 minutes. After you take the couscous out of the *couscousière*, moisten it with cold water and again rub any lumps out of it. Then, season it with salt and pepper, as desired, and add any garniture that you might want, including mint, parsley, cilantro, sautéed red peppers. To make this particular dish, stir in some raisins that have been plumped in water and some toasted almonds.

The Making of Couscous

Semolina flour comes from durum wheat, which is a creamy, yellow-colored wheat. The word "semolina" means "semi-milled," so it has a coarser texture than some other kinds of flour. Couscous begins with two different kinds of semolina flour. Fine semolina is spread in a shallow pan and then moistened. Then, a coarser grind of semolina is sprinkle on top. This mixture is then stirred together. Almost like the process of culturing a pearl, the coarse semolina begins to pick up the fine semolina, which results in tiny beads of pasta. These raw beads of pasta are then steamed until the starches gelatinize. Finally, the couscous is dried. This pre-steamed pasta is what you buy when you buy couscous. All you need to do is rehydrate it and heat it.

Finally, put the couscous back into the *couscousière* for a final steaming of about 20 minutes. It'll come out hot, swollen, tender, and delicate. Cool the couscous with a small amount of water (about a cup of water for a quart of couscous). While the couscous is hot, it will absorb the water readily.

Once the couscous is very light and fully steamed, turn the heat off underneath the *couscousière*. Before you spoon it out onto a plate, add some herbs. When you are ready to plate the couscous, mound it conically onto a plate and make a small divot in the top.

Next, arrange some of the stewed vegetables around the outside of the mound of couscous. Some of the vegetables will be very tender, so be careful that they don't fall apart when you manipulate them. Spoon more of the vegetables, along with some of the broth, into the small divot on top of the couscous. Then, spoon more broth over the couscous, allowing the broth to soak into the couscous to moisten it.

You can serve any extra broth in a separate bowl on the side of the couscous, and if you have extra parsley, sprinkle it on top of the couscous.

Health and Wellness— A Mediterranean Diet

Lesson 10

The Mediterranean diet is one of the healthiest diets in the world. In fact, research has shown that it is protective against all kinds of diseases. In the Mediterranean, while they consume about 40 percent of their calories from fat, that fat is olive oil, which is one of the healthiest fats that exists. In this lesson, you will learn some of the strategies that are used in Mediterranean cooking to make food that is both delicious and healthy.

Fava with Tomato-Braised Capers

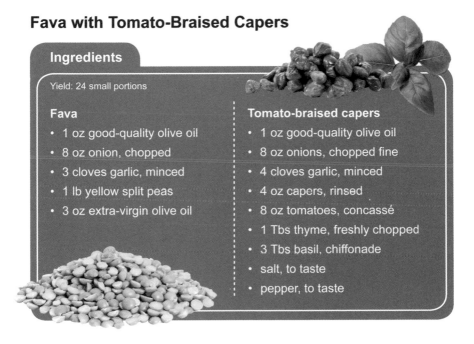

Ingredients

Yield: 24 small portions

Fava
- 1 oz good-quality olive oil
- 8 oz onion, chopped
- 3 cloves garlic, minced
- 1 lb yellow split peas
- 3 oz extra-virgin olive oil

Tomato-braised capers
- 1 oz good-quality olive oil
- 8 oz onions, chopped fine
- 4 cloves garlic, minced
- 4 oz capers, rinsed
- 8 oz tomatoes, concassé
- 1 Tbs thyme, freshly chopped
- 3 Tbs basil, chiffonade
- salt, to taste
- pepper, to taste

To make this dish, begin by cooking some chopped onions and garlic in a pot with olive oil. You want to cook both of them long enough so that they lose their raw flavor—until the onions turn translucent and the garlic becomes aromatic. When this happens, add yellow split peas to the pot, coating them with the flavorful oil. Next, cover the split peas with water and bring them to a boil. Then, reduce the heat and simmer for about an hour to an hour and a quarter.

Eventually, you want the split peas to fall apart into a puree. (Note that when you make a bean puree, often it is called fava even if it's made from a different

bean.) Over time, the split peas will begin to break down. As they do, they will absorb water, so you may need to add water as they cook. But as they get close to being done, be stingy with the water, because you want a dry puree that you can then enrich with olive oil. The dryer they are, the more olive oil you can add, and the more delicious they will taste.

Once the split peas are cooked, add them to a food processor, along with plenty of olive oil, and puree them. Once you are happy with the consistency of the puree, mound some of it onto a plate. Shape the mound with a fork so that it's a little craggy, because you want the crags to capture the capers in the topping you will make for the puree.

To make the tomato-braised capers, start by sweating some onions and garlic (again) in a pan with olive oil. Once the onions become translucent, add some tomatoes (fresh or canned) and some capers to the pan. Then, add some thyme. Turn the temperature down and let the vegetables simmer.

Next, roll a pile of basil into a small cigar and cut it into thin ribbons, which is called a chiffonade, so that it doesn't turn black as its enzymes are exposed to the air. This is the least invasive method of cutting basil.

Season as desired with salt and pepper. The capers probably don't need much salt, if any, because capers are plenty salty. Spoon the tomato-braised capers onto the fava puree, along with a sprinkle of olive oil on top.

Tagine of Salmon with Preserved Lemons and Caper Berries

Ingredients

Yield: 8 servings

Herb mixture
- 8 5-oz salmon
- 1 cup flat-leaf parsley, coarsely chopped
- ½ cup cilantro, coarsely chopped
- 2 Tbs garlic, finely chopped
- ½ cup extra-virgin olive oil
- sea salt, to taste
- 1 ½ tsp black pepper, coarsely ground
- 2 lemons, juiced
- 1 ½ Tbs hot paprika
- ⅛ tsp cayenne pepper
- 1 tsp cumin seed, freshly ground

Vegetable bed
- 12 oz onion, very thinly sliced
- 8 oz fennel, very thinly sliced
- 4 ribs celery, very thinly sliced
- 2 lbs plum tomatoes, split and seeded, large chop
- 2 Tbs garlic, finely chopped
- ⅓ cup caper berries
- 2 preserved lemons, rinsed and slivered
- sea salt, to taste
- black pepper, coarsely ground, to taste
- ⅓ cup extra-virgin olive oil
- ¾ cup water, saffron-infused

To make a salmon *tagine*, start by making a marinade known as *chermoula*. Coarsely chop some parsley and cilantro. Add cumin to this mixture, along with some paprika and cayenne. Then, add some garlic and, finally, olive oil and lemon juice (about three parts oil to one part lemon juice). Mix all of these ingredients together and season the mixture with salt and pepper, as desired. Lay the salmon into the *chermoula* and coat the fish in this marinade.

You're going to cook the fish on a bed of vegetables. Add thinly sliced fennel,

Preserved Lemon

Cultures that don't consume alcohol for religious reasons don't use vinegar—because vinegar is the result of alcohol spoiling. So, how do they make their food sour without vinegar? Lemons are an option, but lemons are seasonal. That's why, in the eastern Mediterranean and North Africa, they discovered the technique of preserving lemon by soaking it in a salt brine.

onion, and celery to a pan. Then, add some tomatoes (fresh or canned, depending on the season). The tomatoes don't need to be peeled or seeded; just cut the core out and dice them up.

Also add some preserved lemon to this mixture. Slowly pull the rind off the meat of the preserved lemon. Then, cut the rind very fine. The rind is salty, but it has a wonderful lemon flavor and none of the bitterness that is associated with lemon rind, because the bitterness has been soaked out of it.

Add some garlic to the mixture and mix all the ingredients together. Then, add some caper berries, which are related to capers. Caper berries and capers can be used interchangeably, so if you can't find caper berries, you can use capers. Slice the caper berries in half.

Lay the fish on top of the bed of vegetables, making sure to add the *chermoula* as well. As this cooks, the vegetables will cook, and the fish will cook and lend its flavor to the vegetables below.

Saffron

Saffron is the stamen from a particular kind of crocus. Out of each blossom comes three threads of saffron. What makes saffron valuable is not only the difficulty of harvesting it, but it also lends a wonderful flavor and color to a dish.

Soak saffron in warm water for as long as you can to get the most flavor and color out of it. It's likely one of the most expensive spices in the world, but a small amount goes a long way, and it stores pretty well, so don't be shy about using it.

Create a sauce by adding some additional ingredients to the pan. First, add saffron-infused water. Then, add some olive oil and a splash of lemon juice.

To speed up the cooking process, put the pan on the stove and bring it to a boil before putting a lid on it and placing it in the oven. Once it's in the oven, cook it for about 25 to 35 minutes at about 375 degrees. The vegetables will become tender, and the moisture will boil, creating steam, which will cook the fish. The juices from the fish will mingle with the vegetable juices below.

Once the fish is cooked, the vegetables are tender, and there's a broth in the bottom that has the color of saffron and tomatoes, pull the salmon out of the oven. Before serving, taste the broth, seasoning it with salt, pepper, or lemon as needed.

Horiatiki Salata, Me Paximadia
(Greek Salad with Barley Rusks, Tomatoes, Cucumbers, Olives, Onions, and Feta)

Ingredients

Yield: 6 portions

- 3 beefsteak tomatoes
- 1 hothouse cucumber, scored, quartered lengthwise, and cut crosswise into ¼-inch dice
- 1 small red onion
- 20 Kalamata olives, pitted and thinly sliced crosswise
- 1 cup feta cheese, diced
- 1 Tbs capers, drained
- 1 tsp dried Greek oregano

- ⅓ cup red wine vinaigrette (olive oil, red wine vinegar, and lemon juice)
- 1 lemon, juiced
- coarse salt, to taste
- black pepper, freshly ground, to taste
- garlic, chopped, to taste
- 3 barley rusks

A Greek salad is a great example of Mediterranean food, because it contains lots of vegetable matter made palatable with lemon juice and olive oil—and not much else. This salad has feta cheese, which is a typical cheese in Greece, but where this Greek salad departs from the Greek salad you're probably familiar with is that the salad rests on top of a barley rusk.

Barley rusk is whole grain barley that is baked into a bread, sliced, and then allowed to dry—or baked until it's completely dry. You're going to rehydrate the barley rusks by pouring some water on top of them and letting them sit for a while in the water. Also add some lemon juice, just so you don't rob it of flavor. Turn the barley rusks in the water until you feel them beginning to soften. You don't want them to fall apart completely. When they are soft, but not too soggy, let them continue to rehydrate out of the water.

To make the dressing, mix olive oil, red wine vinegar, and a little lemon juice. Then, add some dried Greek oregano. Season it with salt and pepper. Also add some chopped garlic that you can turn into a paste.

Next, build the salad. Add olives, cucumbers, red onions, tomatoes, capers, and feta cheese. Toss it together. Taste it to make sure that you like the flavor, adding extra olive oil or seasoning if necessary. If you let the salad sit, it will begin to bleed out some moisture. You might see some on the bottom of the bowl. The barley rusk will absorb all of that flavor.

Break the soft, rehydrated rusks in half and spoon the salad, along with the liquid below the salad, on top of the rusks. This salad can sit in your kitchen for an hour or two until you're ready to eat, and it won't be soupy, because the barley rusks absorb all the extra liquid.

Orange and Date Salad

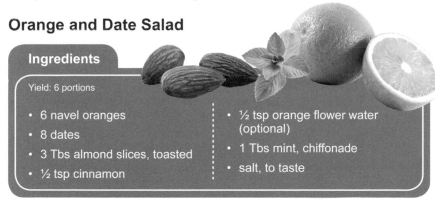

Ingredients

Yield: 6 portions

- 6 navel oranges
- 8 dates
- 3 Tbs almond slices, toasted
- ½ tsp cinnamon

- ½ tsp orange flower water (optional)
- 1 Tbs mint, chiffonade
- salt, to taste

Popular in North Africa, this date and orange salad is a simple fruit salad that can be eaten for dessert. However, in North Africa, this salad would more likely be eaten at the beginning of a meal as a meze, or small dish.

Start with some slices of orange and some dates. Season this mixture with cinnamon, and then add some toasted almonds. An optional ingredient is orange flower water, which is the distilled essence of orange blossoms. If you like the taste of it, add a few drops to the mixture. Season with salt, as desired.

To brighten up the plate, cut some mint into very fine ribbons, or a chiffonade, and add that to the salad as well.

Sharing Abundance—
The Cuisine of Greece

Lesson 11

In this lesson, you will learn about Greek cuisine. Among the high-quality ingredients that are used in Greek cooking, there is an abundance of fresh fruits and vegetables, grains and legumes, alongside a small amount of meat. Simplicity is one of the hallmarks of Greek food, which is prepared from not many ingredients. In this lesson, you will learn how to make a Greek soup called avgolemono, two different kinds of *saganaki*, and a roasted chicken with *horta* and an orzo salad.

Avgolemono

Ingredients

Yield: 4 portions

- 5 cups chicken broth
- ⅓ cup rice
- ¾ cup roasted chicken, shredded

- 3 eggs
- 3 Tbs lemon juice
- salt and pepper, to taste
- branch of oregano, if desired

Avgolemono is a simple, quick egg and lemon soup. To make it, start with some chicken stock in a pot on the stove. Cook some rice (or orzo) in the chicken stock. The rice absorbs the flavor of the chicken, but also the starch of the rice begins thickening the broth and making it more viscous. Add some shredded roasted chicken to the soup and bring it to a simmer.

While the soup comes to a simmer, make what the French call a liaison, which involves binding the soup with eggs and lemon. The yolks of the eggs will thicken slightly, almost as if this were a savory custard, and they will lend a beautiful yellow color and a creamy, velvety texture to the soup. Whip the eggs with some lemon juice.

If you were to take this mixture and put it right into the pot, the protein in the eggs would cook almost immediately, scrambling the eggs and resulting in something akin to an egg drop soup. Instead, you want a velvety, creamy soup. So, you need to temper the heat of the soup before it goes into the eggs by introducing a small amount of hot broth into the eggs while you whisk it.

Once the mixture becomes warm, then you have probably added enough soup to the eggs.

Then, add the liaison—the egg mixture—back into the soup and turn the heat off. You don't want the soup to boil. Stir in the egg mixture for a few minutes. You might notice that the soup will first turn opaque, and then it will start to become velvety and viscous. Taste the soup to make sure you're happy with the flavor.

Season the soup with salt and pepper before serving. Garnish with a branch of oregano, if desired.

Shrimp *Saganaki* with Tomatoes, Oregano, and Feta Cheese

Ingredients

Yield: 4 portions

- 1 ½ lbs large shrimp, shelled and deveined
- ¼ cup olive oil
- 1 cup onion, or 6 scallions, chopped
- 4 garlic cloves, minced
- 2 Tbs oregano
- 1 cup tomato sauce

- 1 cup large tomatoes, peeled, seeded, and diced
- ½ lb feta cheese, crumbled
- 4 Tbs chopped parsley
- 1 tsp salt
- ¼ tsp ground black pepper
- ¼ tsp cayenne pepper (optional)

All of the countries in the Mediterranean seem to have small dishes that you eat at the beginning of a meal, and Greece is no exception. In fact, serving mezes, or *mezethes*, is considered to be an expression of hospitality. *Saganaki*, which refers to an ovenproof dish that these *mezethes* are served in, is common in Greece.

This shrimp-based *saganaki* starts by sautéing shrimp in olive oil. You don't want to cook the shrimp all the way at this point; remove them from the pan once they get some color. After removing the shrimp, the bottom of the pan will be coated with a glaze, which is the flavor of the shrimp concentrated and stuck to the pan. In the same pan, add some more oil. Then, add some onions. The moisture from the onions will help soften the shrimp essence on the pan and allow you to scrape it up.

Once the onions are translucent, add some garlic and continue to cook until the garlic is aromatic. Then, add tomatoes, fresh or canned (or tomato sauce). If you use fresh tomatoes, they should be peeled and seeded before they're chopped up. Season it with a little cayenne and oregano. Also add more olive oil.

Let this sauce cook for three or four minutes, until it gives up some liquid and becomes firmer, more sauce-like. If the shrimp have given off any liquid as they're sitting aside, add the liquid to the sauce. Also add salt and pepper.

Turn the heat down and add the shrimp back to the pan, coating them in the flavorful sauce. As they come in contact with the hot sauce, they'll give up more liquid, so taste the sauce to make sure that you're happy with the flavor as the shrimp cook. Then, add some lemon juice. At this point, the shrimp should be almost fully cooked.

Mound the shrimp in an ovenproof dish. Traditionally, shrimp *saganaki* will be served with some feta cheese sprinkled over the top, and then the dish will be run under the broiler. That last bit of cooking will brown the cheese and cook the shrimp the rest of the way, and the dish will arrive at the table bubbling and hot. Garnish with parsley.

Saganaki (Fried Cheese with Lemon and Olives)

Ingredients

Yield: 8–10 portions

- olive oil for frying
- 1 lb Kefalotyri cheese, ¼-inch thick
- 2 cups water
- 1 cup all-purpose flour

- 1 lemon, juiced
- oregano, to taste
- black pepper, cracked, to taste
- 3 lemon wedges
- 12 Kalamata olives

This is a cheese *saganaki* that uses a type of cheese called Kefalotyri, which is a firm cheese that, when cooked, does not melt. If you can't find Kefalotyri cheese, you can use a Mexican cheese called panela, or there are a number of other cheeses that melt but don't spread.

To make this *saganaki*, heat some olive oil in a sauté pan. After you cut the Kefalotyri cheese, place it in a bowl that has some water in it. Then, lay it in

a bowl with flour. After you dredge the cheese in flour, sauté it. Adding some flour on the outside of the cheese helps guarantee that the cheese does not stick to the pan. Knock off any excess flour, because the excess will burn in the pan. While the cheese doesn't melt, it will become soft, very aromatic, and brown on the outside.

Once the first side of the cheese has browned, flip it and allow the other side to brown as well. Then, add some olives to the pan, just to warm them up. Also add some oregano and pepper. Once the cheese is browned on the second side, put it into an ovenproof dish.

Kefalotyri is relatively salty and a bit gamy. Some people enjoy this cheese with honey drizzled on top. But this version is savory, so instead sprinkle the warmed olives on top. Because this is a rich dish, squeeze some lemon juice on top to lighten it up.

When this cheese *saganaki* is ordered in a restaurant, just before it leaves the kitchen, a little bit of ouzo will be poured over the top of it. Then, when it gets to the dining room, the hot cheese has made the ouzo more aromatic and more volatile, and the server will set a match to it. This technique keeps the cheese soft. As it cools down, it will turn back into a firm cheese.

Roasted Chicken
with *Horta* and Orzo Salad

Ingredients

Kotopolo riganato (roasted chicken with oregano and lemon) Yield: 4 portions

- 1 roasting chicken, 4–5 lbs
- salt, to taste
- pepper, coarsely ground, to taste
- 1 lemon, quartered
- 6 garlic cloves, crushed
- 2 bay leaves
- ¼ cup dried oregano
- ½ cup olive oil
- ¼ cup lemon juice (or to taste)

Horta (Greek boiled greens salad) Yield: 8 portions

- 4 bunches of greens, washed and cut into 2-inch pieces
- mint, cut into ribbons, to taste
- sea salt, to taste
- pepper, to taste

- ½ cup extra-virgin olive oil
- 2 lemons, juiced
- crumbled feta cheese, to taste
- zucchini blossoms, if desired

Orzo salad
Yield: 6 servings

- 8 oz orzo
- 4 oz green lentils
- 1 cup imported green olives, pitted, coarsely chopped
- 1 red bell pepper, roasted, peeled, and cut into long, thin strips
- 4 green onions, chopped
- ⅓ cup extra-virgin olive oil
- 3 Tbs fresh lemon juice
- salt, to taste
- black pepper, freshly ground, to taste
- parsley, chopped, as needed

To make this dish, start by flavoring a chicken with some ingredients that are typical in Greece: garlic, lemon, olive oil, and oregano. Splay the chicken out on a cutting board, and discard of any lumps of fat on the inside of the chicken or any excess skin. Season the chicken, inside and out, with salt and pepper. Then, rub oregano on the outside, and just tuck a bunch of oregano on the inside, without chopping it. Do the same with a few bay leaves. Also rub some chopped garlic on the outside and the inside.

Using some butcher's twine, truss the chicken so that it roasts as evenly as possible. Finally, add some olive oil on top, along with some lemon juice, and roast it in an oven that's preheated at about 450 degrees until it begins to brown. Then, you can turn it down to about 400 or 425. The chicken will be roasted in about 35 to 40 minutes. It's done when the thickest part of the thigh meat reaches an internal temperature of 165 degrees. The chicken should be golden at this point.

Once the chicken comes out of the oven, let it rest underneath a piece of foil, just so that the temperature can reduce, the pressure inside the meat can subside, and the juices can flow back to where they should be.

Raw Chicken

Whenever you're working with raw chicken, be sure to clean your workspace and your hands well afterward.

At its simplest, *horta* is wild greens that are boiled, cooled, squeezed dry, and dressed with olive oil and lemon juice. You can get a variety of greens by buying a braising mix, which is a combination of tougher greens, such as chard, kale, radicchio, beet greens, and black kale. Gather the greens and boil them in salted water. Cook them for about three to five minutes.

While the greens are cooking, assemble a pasta salad that combines grains and legumes, resulting in a complete protein. This pasta salad is made with orzo, which is the pasta that mimics the shape of rice. In a bowl, combine some cooked lentils, roasted peppers, green olives, and green onions.

Make a simple dressing for the orzo salad using salt, pepper, a punchy vegetable olive oil, and lemon juice. You could also add herbs, including chopped parsley. Taste the dressing to make sure that you're happy with the flavor.

Once the greens are just tender enough—barely cooked and still a little crunchy—strain them from the water using a colander in the sink. Cool the greens by splashing some cold water on them. Then, squeeze out the excess liquid. Cut the greens into bite-sized pieces before adding them to a bowl.

Next, add some mint that has been cut into very thin ribbons. Then, add extra-virgin olive oil, lemon juice, salt, pepper, and crumbled feta cheese. You can also add some zucchini blossoms. Finally, toss the salad together, making sure that all the greens are coated with olive oil.

On a large platter, put the *horta* around the edges and the orzo salad in the middle, creating a bed for the stuffed chicken. Before adding the chicken, make sure to cut the strings you trussed the chicken with.

Tastes from the
Palace Kitchens of Istanbul

Lesson 12

Turkey is an interesting country for a number of reasons, including the fact that it straddles three different continents. Historically, Turkey was a center for trade, commerce, and the interchange of ideas. Because it stands at the crossroads of Asia, Africa, and Europe, Turkish cuisine is an expression of the fusion of multiple cultures. As you will learn in this lesson, Turkish meals typically start with mezes and soup, followed by vegetables and fish, and ending with meat and starches.

Yogurt *Çorbasi* (Hot Yogurt Soup)

Ingredients

Yield: 3 pints

- 4 cups whole or low-fat plain yogurt
- ½ tsp salt
- ¼ cup raw medium- or small-grain rice
- 1 qt chicken or lamb stock, degreased
- 1 Tbs cornstarch
- 1 whole egg

- ½ cup milk
- 2 Tbs butter or olive oil
- 1 ½ Tbs dried mint, crumbled
- 1 tsp freshly ground black pepper

To make this soup, start by cooking some rice in chicken stock. You're going to bind, or enrich, this soup with yogurt. But if you simply add yogurt to a hot soup, it will break into a curdy mess. To avoid this, first use cornstarch to create a slurry in some cool water. Dissolve the cornstarch so that there are no lumps. Then, drain some yogurt in a piece of cheesecloth, which causes it to lose the excess whey, little by little. Add the drained yogurt to the slurry of cornstarch and water.

Next, add a whole egg to the cornstarch mixture. (An egg can be problematic, too, because if it gets too hot, it will scramble. So, it can't be added directly to the hot soup.) Also add some milk to the cornstarch mixture. Beat this mixture until it is smooth.

To bring the temperature of the cornstarch mixture closer to the temperature of the soup, temper the cornstarch mixture with hot liquid. Stir in the hot liquid a little bit at a time, incrementally raising the temperature of the yogurt until it is warm, or even as hot as what's in the pot. Once this happens, you can add the cornstarch mixture back to the soup, stir them both together, and put the pot on the heat.

Then, slowly bring the pot up to a boil, which should take about 5 to 10 minutes. Stir it so that everything stays homogeneous. The starch will bind everything together. The starch is not completely cooked until about 185 degrees, so a boil notifies you that it's completely cooked. The egg will also begin to cook, and that will bind the soup. The yogurt should not break or turn curdy. The soup should begin to thicken.

Once the soup comes up to a boil, take the pot off the heat. Taste the soup, seasoning it with salt as needed. When spooning portions of the soup into bowls, make sure that each portion gets some rice, which might be on the bottom of the pot. Finally, drizzle some olive oil on top, along with a sprinkle of dried mint and some black pepper.

Turkish Vegetables Stuffed with Rice

Ingredients

Yield: 10 portions

Rice stuffing
- 1 cup rice
- 2 Tbs currants, soaked
- ¼ cup extra-virgin olive oil
- 2 Tbs pine nuts
- 2 medium onions, finely chopped
- 1 tsp cinnamon, ground
- 1 tsp allspice, ground
- 1 tsp black pepper, ground
- 1 tsp salt
- 1 tsp sugar
- ½ cup hot water
- ½ bunch mint, finely chopped
- 1 bunch dill, finely chopped

Vegetables
- onions
- green and red peppers
- eggplants
- tomatoes
- vegetable or chicken stock, as needed
- olive oil, to taste
- salt, to taste
- pepper, to taste

In Turkey, as well as in Greece, a common practice is to stuff vegetables with flavorful rice. Start with rice that has been soaked in water—about one and a

half times as much water as there is rice—until the rice changes from being translucent to chalky white. Soaking the rice will help it cook more evenly and not break up as it cooks.

Sauté some onions in a hot pan with olive oil. Once the onions turn translucent, flavor them with black pepper, cinnamon, allspice, salt, and sugar. Then, add the rice and its water to the pan. Also add some currants that have been plumped in water. Put a lid on the pan and bring the water up to a boil. Turn the heat down and simmer it until the water is absorbed and the rice is tender.

When the rice is done cooking, pour it out onto a shallow pan and let it cool. Add some toasted pine nuts to the cooked rice, along with chopped dill and mint. Taste the rice, adjusting the seasonings as necessary.

Hollow out a variety of vegetables—including onions, green and red peppers, eggplants, and tomatoes—so that you can stuff them with the rice. In Turkey, chefs will sometimes sauté and season the insides of the vegetables separately, and then add this to the rice.

Season the stuffed vegetables with some salt and pepper, and place them on a pan. Then, pour some liquid—such as vegetable or chicken stock, or even whey from drained yogurt—in the bottom of the pan. Drizzle the vegetables with olive oil before putting them in the oven at about 375 degrees for about 30 to 35 minutes.

Check on the vegetables to make sure that the bottom of the pan does not dry out. Add more liquid as necessary. Once the vegetables are tender, take them out of the oven and serve them at room temperature.

Tomato-Braised Lamb Shanks with Dill and Eggplant Puree

Ingredients

Yield: 4 portions

- 2 lbs lamb shanks
- 1 tsp salt
- ½ tsp ground black pepper
- 6 Tbs olive oil
- ½ cup onion, minced
- 2 garlic cloves, very finely minced
- 3 cups chicken or beef stock
- 4 cups spicy tomato sauce
- ¼ cup dill, chopped
- 2 Tbs parsley, chopped

Hunkar Begendi (Sultan's Delight)

Ingredients

Yield: 6 portions

- 3 globe eggplants, about 1 lb each

Béchamel sauce:
- 2 Tbs butter
- 2 Tbs flour
- 1 cup heavy cream, warmed

- ½ tsp salt
- ¼ tsp ground black pepper
- 1 pinch grated nutmeg

- ½ cup Parmesan cheese, grated

This is a meat dish that would typically be eaten toward the end of a Turkish meal. Start by browning some lamb shanks in a pan with oil. Once they are browned, add some onions, cooking them in the same fat. Turn up the heat and brown the onions. Lightly season with salt and pepper. If you over-season this now, the dish will be too salty if you try to reduce it later. Let the onions take on a deep golden color, and then add some garlic to the pan.

Before the garlic becomes too brown, introduce some chicken or beef stock (or even lamb stock). Then, add some spicy tomato sauce. A rule of thumb is to add liquid so that it comes a third of the way to halfway up the side of the pan of what you're braising. But choosing a pan that is the appropriate size for what you're braising is just as important.

As the liquid comes up to a simmer, put a lid on the pan, and then let it simmer for about an hour and a half, periodically turning the lamb shanks. You know it's done when the meat can be pierced easily with a knife; the knife should also come out easily. You may notice that the meat is so tender that it begins to fall from the bone. If you want to serve the lamb on the bone, then you might want to put a piece of butcher's twine around it to hold the meat tight to the bone. If you want to pull the meat from the bone, then you don't need to do that step.

While the lamb shanks are cooking, make a white sauce to accompany the meat. The white sauce begins with flour and butter, creating what's known as a roux in the French cooking tradition. Stir the flour and butter together in a pan and cook them

Lamb Shanks

Lamb shanks are heavily exercised muscles. The exercise creates a very tough—but also very flavorful—piece of meat. Your challenge as a chef is to make sure that the shanks become tender. To do so, cook them long and slow in a moist environment.

until the raw flavor of the flour has been mitigated—probably about a minute. To test it, take a spoonful out and let it cool, and then run it through your thumb and forefingers. It should feel a little sandy, not smooth the way flour feels.

Next, stir in some half-and-half. As it comes up to a boil, it thickens, and what was a roux is now a semisolid. The starch in the roux has bound to the milk that was added. Add a second batch of half-and-half and stir until it's smooth and thickened. Repeat this process, breaking up any lumps that might form.

When the sauce is between a semisolid and a semiliquid, add the remainder of the half-and-half. Once all the liquid is in, simmer it for about 15 minutes just to make sure that any raw flavor from the flour is no longer apparent. Once the white sauce is made, the French would call it a béchamel.

In the French tradition, when you add cheese to a béchamel, it becomes a Mornay sauce. Add some Parmesan cheese to the sauce and stir it together. Then, add some salt, pepper, and nutmeg. Taste it for flavor. It should have an assertive cheese flavor, and it should be seasoned aggressively because you're going to add eggplant puree to the sauce.

Roast some eggplant over an open flame or under a broiler. Once it's roasted, the pulp on the inside of the eggplant will be very tender and a little smoky. Dig the pulp out of the shell and leave the charred skin behind. Fold the eggplant puree into the sauce and stir. Set this aside.

Check on the lamb shanks. Pierce the meat with a knife. If the knife goes in easily and comes out easily, the meat is done. Once the lamb shanks are done, remove them from the pan. If there's a lot of fat floating on the surface of the sauce that's left in the pan, skim it off. You can also blot the surface with a paper towel. Some fat lends flavor to the sauce, but you don't want too much.

If your sauce is too thin, you can turn up the heat and reduce it. Taste it to make sure you're happy with the flavor, adding salt and black pepper as needed. Also add some dill, which goes well with lamb.

If you want to present the lamb on the bone, you have to handle it very carefully. If you tied twine around the bone to hold the meat in place, remove the tie before serving. If you don't want to serve the lamb on the bone, just ease the bone away from the meat, discarding of any fat or connective tissue you come across. Once the meat has been cleaned up, put it back into the sauce to warm it up.

Spoon the eggplant onto a plate. Then, add the lamb to the plate. Garnish with some chopped parsley.

Poached Apricots Filled with Thick, Drained Yogurt

Ingredients

Yield: 6–8 portions

- 2 cups dried apricots (large if possible)
- 4 cups water
- ¼ cup honey
- 1 cup sugar
- 2 Tbs fresh lemon juice

- 6 cloves
- 2 cinnamon sticks
- 6 cardamom pods, cracked
- 1 cup thick, drained yogurt
- ½ cup pistachios, unsalted, finely chopped

To make this simple Turkish dessert, rehydrate some dried apricots on the stove in a mixture of water, honey, sugar, and lemon juice. Add to the pan some spices, including cardamom, cloves, and cinnamon sticks. Simmer briefly, and then pull them off the heat and allow them to reabsorb the liquid. At this point, the apricots can be refrigerated overnight.

Before they were dried, the apricots were pitted, and you should be able to find a small pocket in each one where the pit used to be. If not, you can cut a pocket into it. Then, fill each apricot with some drained yogurt.

The simplest way to present the apricots would be to sprinkle chopped pistachios on top. Alternatively, you can spoon some of the liquid that they poached in over the top of them.

A Favorite Street Food from the East

Lesson 13

About 10,000 to 12,000 years ago, after the last ice age, our collective nomadic ancestors wandered out of North Africa and into the eastern Mediterranean to find an environment that was perfect for agriculture. Nomadic people cook things simply—often it's meat skewered and cooked over an open flame or vegetables roasted in the dying embers of a fire. Today, some of these simple dishes and techniques are making their way back onto menus in the form of street food. In this lesson, you will learn how to make falafel, an eastern Mediterranean street food, along with some vegetable salads.

Labne with *Dukkah* and *Za'atar*

Ingredients

Labne
Yield: about 32 cheese balls

- 2 lbs thick sheep's milk yogurt
- 3 tsp black pepper, coarsely ground
- 3–4 tsp sea salt
- 2 tsp oregano, dried
- 1 tsp savory or thyme, dried
- 1 small chile, dried, cut in half lengthwise
- 1 bay leaf
- 1 ½–2 cups olive oil

Dukkah
Yield: 4 cups

- 1 cup sesame seeds
- 1 ¾ cup coriander seeds
- ⅔ cup hazelnuts, blanched and skinned
- ½ cup cumin seeds
- 1 tsp sea salt
- ½ tsp pepper, black freshly ground

Za'atar
Yield: 2 ¼ cups

- 8 Tbs sesame seeds
- 12 Tbs fresh thyme leaves, or 8 Tbs dried thyme
- 1 Tbs salt
- 2 tsp black pepper
- 4 Tbs ground sumac

Start with some yogurt that has been mixed with salt and pepper; seasoned with oregano, thyme, chile, and a bay leaf; and then put to drip in a piece of cheesecloth. As the whey drains from the yogurt, the yogurt becomes thicker and thicker. After 24 to 48 hours, it will be thick enough to shape into a simple cheese, and after another 12 hours uncovered in the refrigerator, it will be firm enough to roll into a ball. That cheese is known as *labne*.

The Way to Deal with Extra Whey

The whey that drains from yogurt through a cheesecloth is a valuable ingredient, so don't discard it after making labne. The whey can be utilized in a few different ways. You can cook potatoes in whey, make bread with whey, or even make whey into a refreshing drink.

Roll the cheese balls into some spice mixtures, such as *dukkah* or *za'atar*. Then, dress the cheese balls with olive oil. Serve with pita bread, if desired.

Smoked Eggplant with Yogurt

Ingredients

Yield: 2–4 portions

- 2 large eggplants
- 3 garlic cloves, crushed with salt
- ½ lemon, juiced
- 1 Tbs olive oil

- 2 Tbs yogurt, thick
- 1 tsp salt
- ¼ tsp ground black pepper

To make this salad, fire-roast some eggplant on top of the stove, turning them over an open flame until they collapse. Alternately, put them into a hot oven at about 425 or 450 degrees and let them roast on a pan. You want them to char on the outside and take on a smoky flavor.

Once the eggplant is tender, split its belly open, scoop out the pulp, and put it into a bowl. Because this salad is rustic, it's okay if a piece of the charred skin makes its way into the bowl. Stir the pulp in the bowl, breaking it up as you stir. Then, add some olive oil and lemon juice. Flavor it with garlic that has been mashed into a paste, and season it with salt and pepper.

When the eggplant is relatively smooth, add some drained, thickened yogurt. Whip everything together. Taste it to make sure you're happy with the flavor before serving.

You might think of this as a dip, instead of a salad, but there are many eastern Mediterranean preparations that are very similar to this one that are called salads. For example, you might think of *tzatziki*, which is made of yogurt and cucumbers, as a sauce that you spoon onto food, but it is considered to be a yogurt and cucumber salad in the eastern Mediterranean.

Shredded Beets with Yogurt Sauce

Ingredients

Yield: 6 portions

- 1 pt plain low-fat yogurt
- 8 small beets
- 1 garlic clove, peeled and crushed with
- a pinch of salt

- 2 Tbs lemon juice, fresh
- 1 tsp salt
- ¼ tsp ground black pepper
- ⅛ tsp sugar
- sprig of mint, as needed

This yogurt salad with roasted beets is a similar salad that follows almost the same trajectory as the previous salad, but this salad includes some mint and sugar.

Roast some beets, with the peel intact, in the oven until they're tender. You can tell that they're tender by piercing them with a knife; the knife should go in and pull out easily. Once they're fully cooked, the peel should simply slip off of them. The easy way to peel them is to use a paper towel to rub the skin off the

outside. When peeling beets, wear gloves, unless you want pink hands. Then, trim the stem and the root off.

Next, grate the beets. Add plenty of acid, in the form of lemon juice, to rein in the earthiness of the beets. Then, add some crushed garlic, along with some mint. Also add sugar, which underscores the natural sweetness of the beets. Season it with salt and pepper. Bind the salad with strained yogurt. Stir everything together.

Falafel with Purslane and Tomato Salad

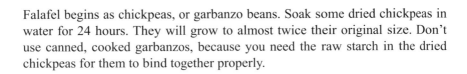

Ingredients

Yield: about 20 balls

Falafel
- 2 cups dried chickpeas
- 2 cups onion, roughly chopped
- ½ cup fresh parsley, finely chopped
- ½ cup fresh cilantro, finely chopped
- 2 tsp salt, or as needed
- ground black pepper, as needed
- 2 tsp dried hot red pepper
- 8 garlic cloves
- 2 tsp cumin
- 2 tsp baking powder
- ½–¾ cup flour (if needed)
- vegetable oil, for frying, as needed

Salad
- purslane, as needed
- 2 tomatoes, for garnish
- 2 onions, diced, for garnish
- 2 green bell peppers, diced, for garnish
- lemon juice, as needed
- extra-virgin olive oil, as needed
- salt, as needed
- pepper, as needed

Tahini sauce
- ½ cup tahini (sesame paste)
- 1 lemon, juiced, or to taste
- ⅓ cup water
- 1–2 garlic cloves, crushed
- ½ cup parsley or cilantro, finely chopped (optional)

- pita bread, as needed

Falafel begins as chickpeas, or garbanzo beans. Soak some dried chickpeas in water for 24 hours. They will grow to almost twice their original size. Don't use canned, cooked garbanzos, because you need the raw starch in the dried chickpeas for them to bind together properly.

Then, drain the chickpeas, making sure to get rid of all the moisture. Add to them chopped onions, whole cloves of garlic, cumin, pepper flakes, parsley, cilantro, salt, and pepper. Grind these ingredients in a food processor for about a minute, being careful not to grind it to a perfectly smooth puree. Stop the food processor once or twice so that you can analyze the texture. It should be slightly granular.

When you're happy with the texture, stop the food processor. Because you want this mixture to be able to bind together into a small ball, you can adjust the consistency by adding a little flour if the mixture is too moist. Falafel can be heavy, which is why you should also add some baking powder. Don't mix it too much; you don't want it to turn into bread dough. You want it to remain tender, not elastic and springy.

Once the flour has been added, taste the mixture to evaluate its salt content, adding more if necessary. Then, see if the mixture holds a loose ball when you form it together. If it's still a little wet, set it aside for about an hour to let the flour absorb the excess moisture.

Next, prepare for frying by filling a pan no more than half full with oil. There needs to be some room for the oil to grow and seethe when you add moist food to it, so don't make the mistake of filling it too full. Alternatively, you can use a tabletop deep-fat fryer. If you have a thermometer, you want the temperature of the oil to be around 350 to 375 degrees.

Using two spoons, shape the chickpea mixture into small egg shapes and then drop them into the oil. Instead of using spoons, you can use an ice cream scoop or roll

Bulgur Wheat: The First Convenience Food

When our ancestors settled in the eastern Mediterranean and embraced agriculture, it was wheat that they were growing and wheat that sustained them. But wheat berries can be pretty hard. You can dry them and store them from one year to the next, but when you try to cook them, they can take hours to get tender. So, our ancestors learned to grind the wheat berries into flour and make bread.

They also came up with the idea to precook or steam the wheat berries until they were tender, and then dry them and crack them. If you were hungry for what is known as bulgur wheat, or precooked wheat, you simply poured boiling water on top of the bulgur wheat and allowed it to rehydrate, and it was ready to eat in about 5 or 10 minutes. Bulgur wheat was one of the first convenience foods, and it had its genesis in the eastern Mediterranean.

the mixture in the palms of your hands. When the balls brown on one side, flip them over. Start to finish, they will fry in about two minutes. Don't overload the oil, because if you do, the balls will take a long time to cook. Instead, fry them in batches.

While the balls are frying, make a simple salad to accompany the falafel. Start with purslane, which is a lemony herb that is used often in a number of different eastern Mediterranean salads. In a bowl, combine purslane that has been washed and plucked into pieces with some cherry tomatoes, diced peppers, and diced red onion. Season with salt and pepper. Splash on some lemon juice and some good-quality extra-virgin olive oil. Mix the ingredients together.

When you're nearly done frying the falafel, turn the heat off under the oil and let the residual heat finish the last few balls. Remove the balls from the oil as they are done frying, sprinkling salt on top as they are still hot.

To make a sandwich with the falafel, start with some pita bread. Tahini sauce—which is sesame paste mixed with garlic, water, and lemon juice— is the traditional sauce to use on falafel. Open up the pita bread and spoon some tahini sauce into it, along with some of the simple salad you made while waiting for the falafel to fry. Finally, add some falafel to the pita, along with more tahini sauce.

Tabbouleh (Bulgur Wheat Salad)

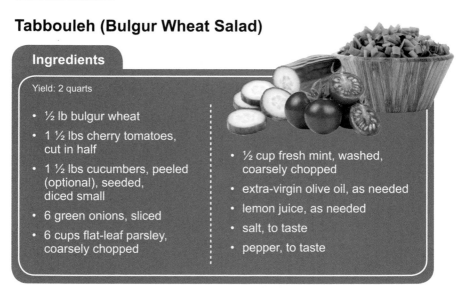

Ingredients

Yield: 2 quarts

- ½ lb bulgur wheat
- 1 ½ lbs cherry tomatoes, cut in half
- 1 ½ lbs cucumbers, peeled (optional), seeded, diced small
- 6 green onions, sliced
- 6 cups flat-leaf parsley, coarsely chopped
- ½ cup fresh mint, washed, coarsely chopped
- extra-virgin olive oil, as needed
- lemon juice, as needed
- salt, to taste
- pepper, to taste

Bulgur wheat (precooked wheat) comes in different grinds, or coarsenesses, but for this dish, use fine bulgur. Pour boiling water over the bulgur, letting it rehydrate for about 10 minutes. Then, drain it and allow it to cool down. It should be tender, moist, and cooked.

In a bowl, add some halved cherry tomatoes, diced cucumbers, and sliced green onions to the bulgur. Also add some mint, which makes the salad bright. Finally, add some chopped parsley. In this dish, parsley is considered to be a vegetable or a salad green, so you want to chop it larger than you usually would. Once you pull the coarse stems out of the parsley, the easiest way to chop a lot of parsley is to gather it into a small, tight ball and chop through it.

Finish the salad with some salt, pepper, lemon juice, and a good-quality extra-virgin olive oil. Stir the ingredients together. There should be just enough bulgur wheat to bind everything together but not so much that this stops being a parsley salad and turns into a bulgur wheat salad.

Tabbouleh is at its best if it can sit for about 15 minutes before you serve it.

Foundations
from the South of France
Lesson 14

As you move toward the south of France, the climate begins to change. At some point, the olive tree begins to thrive, and suddenly you have olives and olive oil. In this region, there is a very different style of cooking from the type of cooking that typically characterizes France. In Paris, cream and butter are used as cooking oils. But in Provence, olive oil is king, and olives are one of the foundational ingredients. In this lesson, you will learn how Provence distinguishes itself from the rest of France by focusing on the olive tree.

Tapenade (Olive Spread)

Ingredients

Yield: 1 ½ pints

- 2 ½ cups black olives, cured, pitted
- ½ cup capers
- ½ cup salted anchovy fillets
- ½ cup extra-virgin olive oil
- ¼ cup lemon juice
- ¼ cup Cognac or dark rum (optional)
- 1 tsp Dijon mustard (optional)
- ground black pepper, to taste
- 1 Tbs parsley

Croûtes (Toast)

Ingredients

Yield: 12–16 portions

- 1 baguette, sliced
- 2 tsp olive oil
- 1 garlic clove, cut

Tapenade is an olive paste that is made with olives, capers, and anchovies. To make tapenade, start by pureeing some cured black olives in a food processor. Add capers and anchovies. Then, add mustard to the food processor and make sure that the puree is smooth. Once it is smooth, add the liquid ingredients, including olive oil and brandy. Then, taste it to determine how much lemon juice it needs. There's no need to add salt, because there's plenty of salt in capers and olives, but you can add some pepper.

Periodically scrape the sides of the inside of the food processor so that you can capture all of the ingredients in the tapenade. You want a sauce that is soft but will hold its shape on a spoon.

Tapenade is a full-flavored condiment that can be used on many different food items. To make it a milder condiment, you can add a can of oil-packed tuna, lentils, or roasted eggplant.

The simplest preparation of tapenade involves spreading it on *croûtes*, or bread that has been brushed with olive oil and garlic and toasted. Alternatively, you can dip breadsticks into the tapenade. A more complex preparation involves spreading the tapenade on a piece of toast, topping with tuna, and sprinkling parsley on top. In fact, you can even garnish deviled eggs with tapenade. After the filling has been piped into the egg white, just add a dollop of tapenade on top.

Vegetable *Tian*

Ingredients

Yield: 8–10 portions

- 1 large onion, julienne
- 1 fennel bulb, julienne
- 1 red pepper, julienne
- ⅓ cup olive oil
- ¼ cup basil, chiffonade
- red wine vinegar, to taste
- 6 zucchini, ¼-inch slices

- 6 Japanese eggplants, ¼-inch slices
- 8 Roma tomatoes, ¼-inch slices
- 2 Tbs thyme, chopped
- 2 Tbs Italian parsley, chopped
- salt and pepper, to taste

The foundation for this vegetable *tian* is a vegetable jam made with onion, fennel, and red pepper. Cook some sliced onions in a pan. Then, add peppers to the pan. Cut the tops off of a fennel bulb, slice it, and then add it to the pan. Season the vegetables with some salt and pepper. Cook them over low heat until they are tender and have wilted down.

Next, create a bed of vegetables in an ovenproof dish. Start by cutting some eggplant, zucchini, and tomatoes into quarter-inch-thick slices and put them into a big bowl. Season the vegetables with salt and pepper. Dress them with olive oil and red wine vinegar. Then, sprinkle on some thyme and parsley. Cut some basil into ribbons, so that it doesn't darken too much, and add the basil to the bowl. Toss all of the ingredients together, making sure that everything is nicely coated and properly seasoned.

Lay the vegetables in an ovenproof dish, alternating the colors of the vegetables. Bake them in the oven at about 400 degrees for about 35 minutes.

The tomatoes will begin to give up their moisture, and they'll start to stew. Then, the zucchini will become tender. Make sure that the eggplant gets cooked all the way through.

In the last 5 to 10 minutes of cooking, you can sprinkle some Parmesan cheese on top of the vegetables, if desired. This dish tastes great at room temperature. It also tastes great as a leftover.

Artichokes *Barigoule*

Ingredients

Yield: 8 servings

- 1 lemon, juiced
- 8 large artichokes
- ⅓ cup extra-virgin olive oil
- 2 oz pancetta or ham, diced (optional)
- 4 garlic cloves, crushed
- 1 fennel bulb, finely sliced
- 1 onion, finely sliced
- 2 carrots, sliced on a bias, about ¼-inch thick

- 1 stalk celery, sliced on a bias, about ¼-inch thick
- kosher salt, to taste
- black pepper, freshly ground, to taste
- 1 ½ cups white wine
- 1 cup water
- 1 bouquet garni (thyme stems, parsley stems, and a bay leaf wrapped in a leek leaf and tied into a bundle)

All about Artichokes

In the Mediterranean, artichokes are weeds that grow wild. In America, people pay a premium for them.

When you're looking for artichokes in the supermarket, you want to buy one that is tightly closed, as opposed to an open blossom. Some artichokes have spines at the end of the leaves, so be careful not to spear yourself. Others are spineless. If you buy artichokes early in the year, it's not uncommon that some will be darkened on the outside if they've been exposed to frost. This is actually preferable; it makes them taste a little better.

Artichokes *barigoule* is a Provençal dish of artichokes that are braised in olive oil and white wine. To make this dish, start by cooking some pancetta in a pan, rendering its fat. To the same pan, add some onions, sliced fennel, and celery and cook them over a very low heat until they wilt, not brown.

When you are dealing with artichokes, you want to have a bowl of acidulated water close by.

Fill a bowl with water and squeeze lemon juice (or vinegar) into it. Artichokes turn brown when they're exposed to oxygen, and dipping artichokes in acidulated water as you work with them will prevent the oxidation of the artichokes.

To access the artichoke heart, pull away and discard some of the coarser dark green leaves from the base of the artichoke. Then, with a sharp paring knife, cut the top half of the artichoke off. Use the knife to pare away the dark green leaves from the outside and the underside. Eventually, you're going to be left with an artichoke heart.

Once the dark green leaves have been peeled away, dip the artichoke into acidulated water. Then, cut the artichoke into quarters, from bottom to top. You will see the purple of the inside. But you will also see what gives an artichoke its name: the choke, which is a very feathery growth that, if left in, can catch in your throat and choke you. Cut the choke out with your paring knife. The purple leaves should come out as well. You will be left with an artichoke heart. After you scrape the artichoke heart clean, put it into the acidulated water.

Repeat this process with the other artichokes. Then, add the artichoke hearts to the pan with the other vegetables. Once the artichokes begin to cook, the enzymes that cause them to brown are destroyed. Also add sliced carrots to the pan. Braise the vegetables in white wine and olive oil.

Once the wine has a chance to reduce, add just enough water to the pan so that you can nestle the artichokes in the liquid but not so much water that the braising liquid loses its savory flavor. Then, add what the French call a bouquet garni, or a garnish bouquet, which is thyme stems, parsley stems, and a bay leaf wrapped in a leek leaf and tied into a bundle. When this preparation is done, it's easy to remove the bouquet garni because it is bundled. Finally, crack a few cloves of garlic and add them to the pan, along with some salt and pepper.

Put a lid on the pan and cook this dish for about 25 to 30 minutes. The artichokes are done when you can pierce the thickest part of an artichoke heart with the tip of a knife and the knife goes in easily but comes out just as easily.

Before serving, drain some of the excess liquid. Drizzle with olive oil, along with a spoonful or two of the braising liquid.

Lamb Chops with *Herbes de Provence*

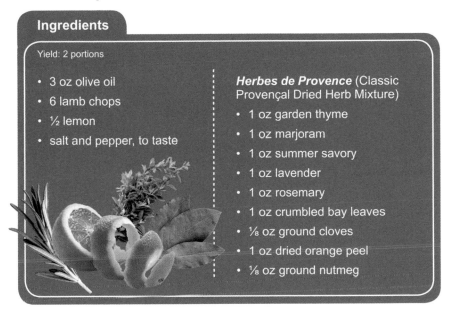

Ingredients

Yield: 2 portions

- 3 oz olive oil
- 6 lamb chops
- ½ lemon
- salt and pepper, to taste

Herbes de Provence (Classic Provençal Dried Herb Mixture)
- 1 oz garden thyme
- 1 oz marjoram
- 1 oz summer savory
- 1 oz lavender
- 1 oz rosemary
- 1 oz crumbled bay leaves
- ⅛ oz ground cloves
- 1 oz dried orange peel
- ⅛ oz ground nutmeg

Provence is famous for its herbs. There is a preparation called *herbes de Provence*, or Provençal herbs, that contains wild thyme, marjoram, bay leaves, lavender, rosemary, savory, orange peel, cloves, and nutmeg.

If you're using fresh herbs, gather them on the branch and put them on a tray in the microwave. When you microwave them, they'll begin to dry out just enough so that if you rub them between your palms, the herb leaves will fall off. This is the easiest way of stripping the leaves from the stems. You can discard the stems. Then, put the mixture into a spice grinder to make it finer.

One of the most popular things to put *herbes de Provence* on is lamb. Start with some lamb chops. Season them with salt, pepper, and *herbes de Provence* on both sides, pressing the spices into the meat and drizzling with olive oil. Let the lamb chops sit for about 20 to 30 minutes.

Cook the lamb chops on a hot grill, making sure that there's enough oil on the outside of the chops. Once they are done cooking, while they're still hot, sprinkle more of the fresh *herbes de Provence* on top so that it's aromatic. Drizzle with lemon juice.

Fruit with Crème Fraîche

Ingredients

Yield: 12–16 portions

- seasonal fruit
- butter, as needed
- crème fraîche, as needed
- brown sugar, as needed
- sprigs of mint, as needed

In Provence—and, indeed, around the Mediterranean—fruit is often consumed as dessert. To make this simple dessert, bake some seasonal fruit (for example, figs, apricots, and blueberries in the summer) under a cap of crème fraîche, which is a cultured cream product that is richer than sour cream.

Start by coating the bottom of an ovenproof dish with butter. Cut the fruit, if necessary, and add them to the dish. Drizzle them with crème fraîche and sprinkle some brown sugar on top.

Place the dish under the broiler. Once the crème fraîche begins to melt, the sugar begins to brown, and the fruit softens, top the dish with some mint and serve.

Fresh Catch—Seafood of the French Riviera

Lesson 15

In this lesson, we're traveling to a region of France known as the French Riviera. Because it's located on the Mediterranean coast, it's no surprise that seafood is a big part of the cuisine in this region. In fact, a fish stew known as bouillabaisse is an iconic dish of the French Riviera, and in this lesson, you'll learn how to make it from scratch, along with a side salad of mixed greens and herbs.

Bouillabaisse (Fish Stew)

Ingredients

Yield: 8–10 portions

- 3 ½–4 lbs mixed fish fillets (i.e., John Dory, red mullet, red snapper, porgy, pompano, striped bass, monkfish, grouper, hake), cut into 3-inch chunks
- ½ cup olive oil
- 1 Tbs pastis aperitif (Ricard or Pernod)
- 1 ½–2 tsp saffron threads, crumbled
- salt, to taste
- ground black pepper, to taste
- lemon juice, to taste
- 2 lbs boiling potatoes, peeled, cut into ½-inch slices
- cayenne pepper, to taste
- 1 baguette or country bread loaf, cut into slices, dried in oven
- 2 garlic cloves, split in half

Fish stock
Yield: 1 gallon

- ¼ cup olive oil
- 2 onions, peeled, minced
- 2 leeks, white only, minced
- 4 garlic cloves, peeled, crushed
- 3 lbs fish bones
- 6–8 plum tomatoes, quartered
- 1 orange or lemon peel, julienne
- 1 celery stalk, cut in pieces
- 3 bay leaves
- 2 tsp pastis aperitif or wine
- 2 thyme sprigs
- ¼ tsp cayenne pepper
- salt, to taste
- ground black pepper, to taste
- 1 gallon water, boiling

To make this dish, start by making a fish stock. When you make generic fish stock, you want to keep it neutral so that you can use it in many different dishes. However, this fish stock is only going to be used to craft the bouillabaisse, so it will be pretty distinctive.

In a pot on the stove, sweat some onions, leeks, celery, and garlic in olive oil. Cook them long and slow so that they collapse and become very sweet. Add fish bones, such as those from a branzino, breaking them a few times before adding them. You can put the head in as well—just don't add the guts of the fish. Turn the heat up a little.

Fish in the South of France

Bouillabaisse utilizes the seafood that the fishermen in the south of France catch, and it's not just familiar fish, such as salmon, shrimp, and halibut. It's all kinds of fish, some of which don't have much meat but a lot of bone, and it's the bones of the fish that give the soup its distinctive flavor and texture.

Because many of the fish that you would add to a bouillabaisse in the south of France might not be available to you, you might have to make some substitutions. Use whatever good-quality fish is available to you. And all the fish will have bones that you can use to flavor the bouillabaisse.

One of the secrets to a good fish stock is to sweat the bones so that they begin to turn opaque, and they will fall apart and separate from each other within about 10 to 12 minutes. The volume will be reduced by about a third to a half, and then you only need to add half as much water to cover the bones. This results in the concentration of flavor in the broth.

Once the bones begin to fall apart, add some white wine and turn the heat up, allowing the wine to reduce for a minute or two. This is the only opportunity for you to concentrate the flavor of the wine in the absence of other liquid. You want the acidity of the wine to be the backbone of your stock.

Once the wine has reduced, add some tomatoes (fresh or canned). Then, add some orange zest, thyme, bay leaves, and cayenne pepper. Next, add hot water to the pot, making sure the bones are covered, and allow it to simmer. Fish bones are delicate and give up their flavor in about 20 to 30 minutes.

Once the bones have completely fallen apart and the vegetables have cooked down, strain the bones from the liquid. Using a ladle, put the stock through a fine sieve. Discard the bones. Then, taste the fish stock and season with salt and pepper.

If you are making the bouillabaisse today, the stock is ready. If you're going to wait until tomorrow, make sure that the stock is cooled quickly and then immediately refrigerated, because seafood spoils quickly.

To prepare for the bouillabaisse, soak some saffron in hot water. The color will come out of the saffron and make its way into the water. After it soaks, add the saffron to some fish fillets (such as a combination of monkfish, branzino, and sea bass) that have been cut up into chunks. Let this sit in the refrigerator for an hour or two. If you made your stock a day ahead, marinate the seafood overnight. It'll keep better, but it'll also garner more flavor.

To make bouillabaisse, start by putting the fish stock in a pan and bring it up to a simmer. Then, add some potatoes cut into wedges. Bring it up to a boil, and then allow the potatoes to cook for about 15 minutes, or until they can be pierced easily with a knife.

Next, add some olive oil and pastis (Pernod), which is an aniseed-flavored aperitif wine that has a strong liquorish flavor. Be careful not to add too much, because the flavor can be overwhelming. Then, squeeze some lemon juice into the pan. At this point, taste it and add more salt, cayenne pepper, lemon juice, or Pernod as desired. Take the time to get the flavoring right.

Once the fish has been marinated with saffron for an hour or two, add it to the hot broth. By the time the broth comes back up to a simmer, it will most likely be done. Taste it once more and adjust the flavor as necessary.

Serve this soup with some croutons that have been toasted and rubbed with garlic.

Rouille (Garlic and Saffron Mayonnaise)

Ingredients

Yield: 8 ounces

- 2 cayenne chiles
- 3 garlic cloves
- ¼ tsp kosher salt
- ½ tsp saffron, powdered, dissolved in 1 Tbs boiling water
- ¼ tsp fresh bread crumbs

- 1 egg yolk, room temperature, or 1 Tbs pasteurized egg yolk
- 1 tsp lemon juice
- 1 cup olive oil, room temperature

Rouille, which starts out as a garlic mayonnaise, is a great garnish for bouillabaisse. Start by placing some garlic in a mortar, along with a little salt. Then, pound it into a paste. Also add some dissolved saffron and bread crumbs, and again pound into a paste.

Next, mix in an egg yolk. Ultimately, you're going to try to mix two things that don't like to mix: olive oil and water. You're going to take advantage of an egg yolk, which has an emulsifier called lecithin that will help bind these two disparate ingredients together.

Initially, mix in the olive oil drop by drop, very slowly, until you've established an emulsion. This mixture should never look oily; it should always look a little creamy. If it ever looks slick and greasy, it's indicative of mixing too quickly, so slow down.

Once the mixture starts to become thick, that's indicative of the emulsion beginning to form. Add a drop or two of lemon juice, and then carry on with the oil. Once the emulsion has formed, you can be more cavalier about how quickly you add the oil.

Taste it to assess the flavor. Salt has already been added, but at this point, you can add more, if necessary, along with some cayenne pepper. Also add more lemon juice.

You can spoon the rouille over the garlic toasts you prepared for the bouillabaisse and then add the toasts to the soup when you are ready to serve it. If you have extra rouille, put it in a small bowl and place it on the table so that guests can add it to the soup according to their own taste.

Mixed Salad with Herbs

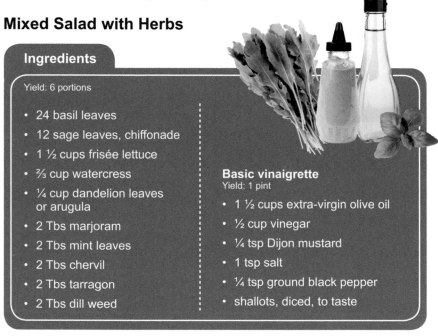

Ingredients

Yield: 6 portions

- 24 basil leaves
- 12 sage leaves, chiffonade
- 1 ½ cups frisée lettuce
- ⅔ cup watercress
- ¼ cup dandelion leaves or arugula
- 2 Tbs marjoram
- 2 Tbs mint leaves
- 2 Tbs chervil
- 2 Tbs tarragon
- 2 Tbs dill weed

Basic vinaigrette
Yield: 1 pint

- 1 ½ cups extra-virgin olive oil
- ½ cup vinegar
- ¼ tsp Dijon mustard
- 1 tsp salt
- ¼ tsp ground black pepper
- shallots, diced, to taste

Make a salad to go with the bouillabaisse. Gather a range of greens and herbs, such as basil, sage, frisée, watercress, dandelion leaves (or arugula), marjoram, mint leaves, chervil, tarragon, and dill weed. Other options include blossoms from garlic chives, radicchio, escarole, celery leaves, parsley, lovage, sorrel, purslane, zucchini flowers, nasturtiums, romaine, salad burnet, and borage flowers. Take some time to choose the greens that go into this salad.

When you make a salad, soak it in cold water—or even ice water—and let it crisp up for about 10 to 15 minutes. Then, refrigerate the salad for about 30 minutes before you're ready to eat it.

Next, make a simple salad dressing. Put some diced shallots into a jar. Add Dijon mustard to the jar, along with some vinegar and olive oil. Shake it until it is thoroughly mixed. Then, season the dressing with salt and pepper, keeping in mind that it should be aggressively seasoned because it has to flavor so much greenery.

When you are ready to serve, arrange the salad on a platter and gently ladle the dressing on top. It's better to use less salad dressing and bring a bowl of it to the table with you than to use too much, resulting in lettuce that is matted together and wilted.

Bringing the Mediterranean Home

Lesson 16

O live oil is pervasive around the Mediterranean—and for good reasons. The olive tree thrives in the Mediterranean climate, and the calories associated with olive oil have sustained the people of the region for thousands of years. In modern times, olive oil has been discovered to be a nutritional powerhouse. In fact, it is one of the healthiest fats you can consume. In this lesson, you will explore different ways to incorporate olive oil into your culinary life.

Toasted Bread with Marmalade, Olive Oil, and Salt

Ingredients

Yield: 10 portions

- 10 slices rustic peasant bread
- ½ cup extra-virgin olive oil, robust
- 1 cup orange marmalade, bitter
- 1 oz sea salt

Breakfast in the Mediterranean

In many countries in the Mediterranean, breakfast does not involve sweet food. Instead, it consists of savory food, including meats, cheeses, tomatoes, peppers, olives, and good-quality bread. And olive oil is entirely appropriate for breakfast, regardless of whether you're eating a sweet or savory breakfast.

One of the best ways to really appreciate the flavor profile of olive oil is pairing it with some toast and marmalade. Slice some whole-grain bread, toast it, and then spread a bitter marmalade on it. Then, drizzle a pungent, punchy olive oil on top. The olive oil provides richness and gives the marmalade a depth of flavor it didn't have before. Finally, sprinkle some good-quality sea salt, such as flaky Maldon salt, on top.

An alternative to this recipe uses rye toast with avocado spread on it, along with olive oil, salt, and pepper. You can also cook an egg in olive oil, as an alternative to butter, and eat it with some toast for breakfast.

Brandade of Fennel and Celeriac

Ingredients

Yield: 8 portions

- 3 lbs celeriac, peeled, quartered
- 3 lbs fennel, cored, quartered
- 2 lbs potatoes, russet, peeled, quartered
- 8 cloves garlic, minced
- ⅔ cup olive oil

- 1 ⅓ cup cream
- ½ tsp star anise, ground
- salt, to taste
- ground black pepper, to taste
- ½ cup parsley, chopped
- lemon juice, to taste

In a pan on the stove, sauté some garlic in olive oil. Then, add some star anise and cream. Let the cream come up to a simmer, and then turn the heat down and let it reduce by about half. Then, taste it to determine how much salt and pepper to add.

Boil some potatoes, celery root, and fennel in salted water until they are tender. Then, take them out and allow them to steam dry. You want to get rid of most

of the excess water. Put the vegetables into a food mill and puree them. Once all that's left in the food mill is the fiber from the fennel, remove the vegetables from the food mill.

Stir some cream into the vegetable puree. But don't be too overzealous with the cream. This should be a mousse-like consistency; it should not turn into soup. Then, brighten it up with some lemon juice. Finally, add some chopped parsley.

Mound the brandade onto a small plate. You can serve it warm, but it is also delicious at room temperature. You can also drizzle a little extra cream over the top. Serve with toast, if desired.

Roasted Tomato and Saffron Vinaigrette

This salad dressing incorporates the flavor profile of a complex bouillabaisse into a simple vinaigrette. To make this dressing, start by roasting some tomatoes until the flesh collapses. Then, peel away the blackest parts of the skin and chop them up. Add them to a bowl.

Next, add some mustard, which acts as an emulsifier. Also add some saffron that has been soaked in water. Then, add garlic, shallots, thyme, salt, pepper,

Ingredients

Yield: 3 cups

- 4 Roma tomatoes, roasted and peeled
- 2 Tbs shallots, minced
- 2 cloves garlic, minced
- 1 Tbs Dijon mustard
- ¼ cup red wine vinegar
- 1 orange, juiced and zested
- ¼–½ tsp saffron, soaked in 1 oz water
- 1 Tbs Pernod
- ¾ cup extra-virgin olive oil, French
- 1 tsp thyme, chopped
- 1 Tbs capers, chopped
- coarse salt, to taste
- black pepper, freshly ground, to taste
- pepper flakes, to taste (optional)

and even a few pepper flakes to give it a punch. Chop some capers and add them to the bowl as well.

For this to become a vinaigrette, you need to add vinegar and oil. So, add some red wine vinegar and olive oil. Then, add orange zest, along with some orange juice, to the vinaigrette. Finally, add some Pernod, or aniseed-flavored aperitif wine. Taste the vinaigrette to determine if it needs any extra seasoning.

This is an all-purpose vinaigrette that you can use on fish, shellfish, poultry, or vegetables. It also keeps very well in the refrigerator.

Warm Salad of Curly Endive with Braised Artichokes and Goat Cheese

Ingredients

Yield: 8 portions

Braised artichokes

- 4 large artichoke hearts, cut into eighths
- 1 small onion, julienne
- 4 garlic cloves, sliced thin
- 1 small carrot, peeled and sliced 1/16-inch thick
- ½ cup extra-virgin olive oil
- ⅓ cup fennel, cut ¼ inch by 2 inches
- 1 orange, juiced and zested
- ¾ cup dry white wine
- 4 branches fresh thyme
- 2 bay leaves
- salt, to taste
- ¼ tsp black pepper, freshly ground

Dressing

- ⅔ cup braising liquid, reserved from the artichokes
- 2 Tbs red wine vinegar
- 1 tsp fresh thyme leaves
- 3 oz fresh goat cheese
- salt, to taste
- ¼ tsp ground black pepper

Salad

- 1 head curly endive (frisée), cleaned and cut into bite-sized pieces
- ⅔ cup celery leaves
- ½ cup Italian parsley leaves
- 32 asparagus tips, blanched
- 6 radishes, sliced thin
- ¼ cup fennel tops
- 3 oz fresh goat cheese, broken into chickpea-sized pieces
- salt, to taste
- ½ tsp black pepper, freshly ground

A great accompaniment to the roasted tomato and saffron vinagraitte—served with chicken, for example—would be artichokes *barigoule*, or braised artichokes in white wine with olive oil and aromatic vegetables. You can either repurpose artichokes *barigoule*, which you might have left over from Lesson 14, or you can braise some artichokes according to this recipe.

In Mediterranean cuisine, if anything can be repurposed, it should be repurposed. The braising liquid that the artichokes were cooked in—which contains good-quality olive oil, white wine, herbs, garlic, and flavor from various vegetables—can be made into a warm salad dressing.

Start by adding the braising liquid from the artichokes to a warm pan and bring it up to a boil. Flavor it by adding some thyme and vinegar. Then, season it with salt and pepper. Allow the braising liquid to simmer for a short amount of time so that the flavor of the thyme can make its way into the broth.

Once the braising liquid comes up to a simmer, taste it to make sure that you're happy with the flavor. Then, stir goat cheese into the liquid. You want to add enough goat cheese so that you're happy with the flavor but also with the texture. It should become viscous, the way you would expect a salad dressing to be, but also creamy.

Because this is a warm dressing, the salad that this dressing will go on should include greens that can withstand heat, such as curly endive (frisée) or escarole. For this salad, cut some curly endive into bite-sized pieces. Add some celery leaves and parsley leaves. You can also add some Belgian endive and radicchio for color. Then, add some asparagus tips and sliced radishes. If you have leftover goat cheese, break it in small lumps, about the size of a chickpea or an olive, and add it to the salad. Season with salt and pepper.

Pour the warm, creamy dressing over the salad and toss all of the ingredients together. Add some fennel tops to the salad as a garnish.

Mediterranean Desserts

Pedro Ximénez (PX) is a dessert wine that is vinified from grapes of the same name. But when these grapes are harvested, they are allowed to dry in the sun and "raisin" for about a week before the grapes are vinified into wine. This results in a rich, raisiny wine that is fortified to about 22 percent alcohol. It also has a nuttiness that is indicative of a sherry that has gone through oxidative aging.

One of the best ways to enjoy this wine is poured over ice cream. Flavors of ice cream that would complement this wine well include vanilla ice cream (with a cookie on the side), almond ice cream (topped with almonds), pistachio ice cream (garnished with toasted, salted pistachios), and coffee ice cream (topped with coffee beans coated in chocolate and then cocoa powder).

Sweets look very different in the Mediterranean. Often, meals are finished with dried fruit or fresh fruit. If it involves pastries or a sweet of some kind, the portions are small. And they use whatever is available. This is a very simple dessert that takes advantage of sherry and some ice cream that you might already have in your freezer.

Bibliography

Mediterranean

Davidson, Alan. *Mediterranean Seafood*. Berkeley, CA: Ten Speed Press, 2002.

Helou, Anissa. *Mediterranean Street Food*. New York: William Morrow, 2006.

Jenkins, Nancy Harmon. *The New Mediterranean Diet Cookbook*. New York: Random House, 2012.

Weir, Joanne. *From Tapas to Meze*. New York: Crown, 1994.

Wolfert, Paula. *Mediterranean Cooking*. New York: William Morrow, 1994.

Italy

Batali, Mario. *Simple Italian Food*. New York: Clarkson Potter, 1998.

Hazan, Marcella. *Essentials of Classic Italian Cooking*. New York: Knopf, 2011.

Root, Waverly. *The Food of Italy*. New York, Vintage, 1992.

Spain

Casado, Matt A. *Spanish Cuisine*. Hoboken, NJ: John Wiley & Sons, 1997.

Casas, Penelope. *The Food and Wine of Spain*. New York: Knopf, 1982.

Dunlap, Fiona. *New Tapas*. London: Mitchell Beazley, 2002.

France

Ducasse, Alain. *Flavors of France*. Muskogee, OK: Artisan, 1998.

Freson, Robert. *Taste of France*. New York: Stewart, Tabori & Chang, 2001.

Peterson, James. *Glorious French Food*. Hoboken, NJ: John Wiley & Sons, 2002.

Greece

Barron, Rosemary. *Meze: Small Bites, Big Flavors*. San Francisco, CA: Chronicle Books, 2002.

Kochilas, Diane. *The Food and Wine of Greece*. New York: St. Martin's Press, 1993.

Salaman, Rena. *Greek Food*. New York: Fontana, 1983.

Turkey

Algar, Ayla. *Classical Turkish Cooking*. New York: HarperCollins, 1991.

Basan, Ghillie. *Classic Turkish Cooking*. London: I. B. Tauris, 2012.

Eren, Nesret. *Art of Turkish Cooking*. New York: Hippocrene Books, 1993.

Morocco, Tunisia, and North Africa

Carrier, Robert. *A Taste of Morocco*. New York: Clarkson Potter, 1987.

Hafner, Dorinda. *A Taste of Africa*. New York: Ten Speed Press, 2002.

Wolfert, Paula. *Couscous and Other Good Food from Morocco*. New York: Ecco, 1987.

General References

Note: The following books are available on the website of The Culinary Institute of America at http://www.ciaprochef.com/fbi/.

Conniff-Dobrich, Cate. *Seasons in the Wine Country: Recipes from The Culinary Institute of America at Greystone.* San Francisco: Chronicle Books, 2010.

The Culinary Institute of America (CIA). *Breakfasts and Brunches.* New York: Lebhar-Friedman, 2005.

————. *Cooking at Home with The Culinary Institute of America.* New York: Wiley, 2003.

————. *The Culinary Institute of America Cookbook: A Collection of Our Favorite Recipes for the Home Chef.* New York: Lebhar-Friedman, 2008.

————. *Gourmet Meals in Minutes.* New York: Lebhar-Friedman, 2004.

————. *Grilling: Exciting International Flavors from the World's Premier Culinary College.* New York: Lebhar-Friedman, 2006.

————. *Healthy Cooking at Home with The Culinary Institute of America.* New York: Wiley, 2011.

————. *The New Book of Soups.* New York: Lebhar-Friedman, 2009.

————. *One Dish Meals.* New York: Lebhar-Friedman, 2006.

————. *Pasta: Classic and Contemporary Pasta, Risotto, Crespelle, and Polenta Recipes.* Hoboken, NJ: John Wiley & Sons, 2013.

————. *The Professional Chef.* 9th ed. New York: Wiley, 2001. (The online version of this book can be found at https://www.inkling.com/store/professional-chef-cia-9th/.)

————. *Vegetables.* New York: Lebhar-Friedman, 2007.

————, Mark Erickson, and Lisa Erickson. *Cooking for One: A Seasonal Guide to the Pleasure of Preparing Delicious Meals for Yourself.* New York: Lebhar-Friedman, 2011.

———— and Ben Fink. *Hors d'oeuvre at Home with The Culinary Institute of America*. New York: Wiley, 2007.

———— and Lynne Gigliotti. *Mediterranean Cooking*. Boston: Houghton Mifflin Harcourt, 2013.

———— and Abigail Kirsch. *Entertaining: Recipes and Inspirations for Gathering with Family and Friends*. Hoboken, NJ: John Wiley & Sons, 2012.

———— and Katherine Polenz. *Vegetarian Cooking at Home with The Culinary Institute of America*. New York: Wiley, 2012.

————, Gianni Scappin, Alberto Vanoli, and Steven Kolpan. *Italian Cooking at Home with The Culinary Institute of America*. New York: Wiley, 2011.

———— and Martha Rose Shulman. *Culinary Boot Camp: Five Days of Basic Training at The Culinary Institute of America*. New York: Wiley, 2006.

Fischer, John W., and Lou Jones. *Bistros and Brasseries: Recipes and Reflections on Classic Café Cooking*. New York: Lebhar-Friedman, 2008.

Scappin, Gianni, and Vincenzo Lauria. *A Tavola! Recipes and Reflections on Traditional Italian Home Cooking*. New York: Lebhar-Friedman, 2009.

Shulman, Martha Rose. *Spain and the World Table*. New York: DK Adult, 2011.

Recipe List

Photographic Credits

Notes